The Casey Martin Story

Walk A Mile In My Shoes

The Casey Martin Story

Walk A Mile In My Shoes

Tom Cunneff

Rutledge Hill Press®

Nashville, Tennessee

Published in Nashville, Tennessee, by Rutledge Hill Press®, 211 Seventh Avenue North, Nashville, Tennessee 37219.

Distributed in Canada by H. B. Fenn & Company, Ltd., 34 Nixon Road, Bolton, Ontario L7E 1W2.

Distributed in Australia by The Five Mile Press Pty., Ltd., 22 Summit Road, Noble Park, Victoria 3174.

Distributed in New Zealand by Tandem Press, 2 Rugby Road, Birkenhead, Auckland 10.

Distributed in the United Kingdom by Verulam Publishing, Ltd., 152a Park Street Lane, Park Street, St. Albans, Hertfordshire AL2 2AU.

Typography by Compass Communications, Inc., Nashville, Tennessee

ISBN: 1-55853-686-8
Library of Congress Cataloging-in-Publication Data available

Printed in the United States of America

1 2 3 4 5 6 7 8 9—02 01 00 99 98

For my parents,
Shirley and Ray Cunneff

CONTENTS

PREFACE

Any good story is character driven, and this one is no different. Casey Martin was born a natural athlete, but he was also born with a crippling disease. Talk about cruel: It's like getting a Formula One race car and then not having any gas. From the time Martin was a baby, his life has been one of dealing with excruciating pain and overcoming obstacles. But never once did he complain or make excuses for himself or hide behind his disability. In fact, he at first refused to admit he even had one. He was stubborn to a fault. He didn't want anyone's help. But he changed. Not only did he eventually admit to himself that he was disabled, he finally asked for help and then he demanded it in a court of law.

When my editor at Rutledge Hill Press, Mike Towle, first brought this project to me through my agent, Scott Waxman, I was naturally excited. Not just because I had an opportunity to write in-depth about a sport I enjoy so much, but also because Martin's story transcends golf into much larger societal issues. Forgive the expression, but this one had legs. Unlike most articles I had written, length didn't constrict me. I was eager to explore every facet, nook, and cranny of Martin's life. Mike and Scott have my deepest gratitude for giving me the opportunity to go on a new journey, which, to me, is what being a journalist is all about.

I was full of trepidation when I began the book. Though the title of this book has the word "My" in it, I want to make it perfectly clear that Casey Martin would have nothing to do with it. Yet the Martin family is a class act. Even though they were involved in Casey's own book project, they didn't try to thwart me. As King Martin told me, "We're not in this thing for the money." I believe him. Still, while I had reported many "unauthorized" profiles in my ten years as an L.A.-based staff correspondent at *People* magazine, doing a whole book on someone without their direct involvement seemed daunting, especially since I had less than two months' time in which to do it.

First, I had to get some time off from *People* and permission to do the book. Obviously, I got both. To that end, many thanks go to managing editor Carol Wallace, assistant managing editor Joe Treen, and West Coast Bureau chief Jack Kelley.

After gathering just about every magazine article written on Martin (with many thanks to my friend at *Golf World,* Mike Arkush, for his help), I commenced my reporting task in early April in Martin's hometown of Eugene, Oregon. Fortunately, he lived in just the right-sized town: big enough to warrant a first-rate paper, the *Register-Guard,* but not so big that the paper didn't cover high school golf. I spent hours at the town library calling up clips, not just from the trial itself, but many others detailing Martin's high school and amateur golf career. The paper knew a good story when it saw one, so Martin was accorded a lot of coverage. The articles proved invaluable in building a framework to reconstruct his very formative teenage years.

Also of help were the folks at South Eugene High School, who gave me access to the yearbooks from those years Martin was a student there. Gathering the names of his teammates and doing a little rudimentary detective work to reach them, I was able to start filling in the gaps that are inevitably there in even the best newspaper and magazine pieces. His old friends were more than happy to talk about Casey since they all liked him so much. Finding them was a little problematic given that many of them have left Eugene. Locating one, however, usually led to another one and then another. When that hit a wall, there was always the Internet. People-finder Web sites make life so much easier for any investigation like this. I found the home phone numbers on the Web for perhaps my two best sources, Casey's Hooters Tour buddy Bill Hoefle and Casey's childhood friend Joel Rubenstein, who, it turned out, lived just a mile or two from my home in Marina del Rey, California. Small world. Thank you both for your candor and your contacts.

I also want to thank my research associate at Stanford, Dana Mulhauser, who turned up dozens of clips from the *Stanford Daily* on the golf team during Martin's tenure. What was strange, though, was the complete lack of reference to his leg problem, which worsened considerably while in college. It was almost as if the paper purposely avoided mentioning it. His coach and teammates also closed ranks around him when I tried to interview them. But coupled with other articles and interviews, I was able to get a good feeling for his time there, during which he led the team to an NCAA title—and this was the year before Tiger Woods joined the squad. Having the best golfer in the game as his college teammate just added another layer and element to a story full of them. Woods was already a media sensation when he arrived at "the Farm," as the campus is called, but who could have guessed that Martin would rival him one day in press attention?

Given Martin's success in college and the fact that he was allowed to use a cart, I'm surprised the PGA Tour didn't see a lawsuit like Martin's coming. Then again, what could they have done? The tour's cart policy is so flexible someone was bound to challenge it sooner or later. Whittling down one thousand pages of trial transcripts to fifty or so was no easy task, but it was much more involving than I imagined, since I learned about everything from the intricacies of litigation to how the players collect their winnings.

Golf is a game of opposites, and so was the case itself. In one corner you had a very sympathetic and talented individual who just wanted to pursue his dream, a dream he had worked so hard at achieving; in the other corner you had an amorphous and rigid organization that was determined to protect its way of life. On the surface, it seemed like a no-brainer: Give the guy a cart. These are the nineties after all, not the fifties. But it wasn't so black and white. Even King Martin admitted he could see where the PGA Tour was coming from in their absolute belief that allowing Casey to use a cart could severely impact their competitions.

Before I began this book I could understand where both sides were coming from. However, once I started reporting the book and grasped just how painful and debilitating Martin's disease is, as well as the law under which he sued, I became more convinced than ever that the court's decision was the right one. The Americans with Disabilities Act is the law of the land and supersedes the tour's cart-ban rule, at least as far as the disabled are concern. Moreover, carts aren't against the general rules of golf as set forth by the United States Golf

Association. There's no way that Martin's use of a cart even comes close to giving him an advantage. My respect for Martin has only grown. He seems to have handled the attention as well as anybody could. He has always kept things in perspective; having a dying leg will tend to do that.

Finally, I don't know how anybody could do a book like this and not come away with better appreciation for the things in our lives that we take for granted. It's trite but true. Casey's disability makes life's simplest tasks, such as taking a shower or driving a car, even sleeping, seem monumental. If you think your life is difficult, it's not, not until your legs or your arms or your eyes don't work. The disabled have a saying for people with healthy bodies. They call us "temporarily able-bodied." I'll always try to remember that.

Introduction

At 8:33 A.M. on March 2, 1998, Casey Martin teed up his Top-Flight Strata golf ball on the first hole of the Hills Country Club in Austin, Texas. A huge crowd gathered around the tee box on the unusually warm and muggy day. Martin took a few practice swings, nestled his Great Big Bertha driver behind the ball, and then ripped it—straight into the rough on the 454-yard par-four opening hole. No matter. He could have skulled the shot and it still would have been one of the most significant golf shots ever hit: It was Martin's first competitive stroke since scoring the biggest victory of his young life a month earlier. Living out a classic David vs. Goliath story, he had taken on the PGA Tour and won the right to ride a cart in competition. Martin, hobbled by an incurable and degenerative circulatory disorder in his right leg that makes walking difficult and painful, sued the tour under the Americans with Disabilities Act (ADA) for the right to use a cart in competition on the Nike Tour.

The case ignited a host of controversies, ranging from the very definition of the game of golf to the rights of the disabled. The Casey Martin case took golf from the sports page to the front page, and was the subject of seemingly endless discussion

15

from political talk shows to golf course grillrooms across the country. No one, it seemed, was without an opinion on the landmark case. As Martin and another player rode in the back of a cab from the airport to play in the Nike Tour's Greater Austin Open, the driver asked them, "So, what do you think about the guy getting to ride in a cart?" Martin just smiled sheepishly and said, "Well, that's me." The driver looked over his shoulder in surprise, and the questions stopped.

What made the case so fascinating was that Martin was doing what millions of golfers do every day: hit a ball, hop in a cart, and hit it again. Only in this rare case, here was a golfer, indeed a very good one, who was suing to drive his cart onto the sacred turf of golf's most competitive arena—the PGA Tour and its offshoot Nike Tour. The PGA Tour, however, was determined to do everything to stop him, even bringing in such legendary names as Nicklaus and Palmer to testify on its behalf against a relatively unknown, twenty-five-year-old aspiring golf pro. It just so happened that Casey Martin emerged quickly to be hailed as a role model for a disabled demographic that numbers forty-five million Americans. In a game where the difference between picking up range balls for a living and picking up first-place checks can be only a couple shots per round, the tour forcefully argued that giving Martin use of a cart would give him an unfair advantage and, therefore, substantially alter the game.

Even when the case was finally behind him, the media scrutiny was not. One hundred eighty members of the media (up from the usual twenty-five or so at a typical Nike Tour stop) gathered in Austin to witness Martin's historic round. The media room wasn't big enough to accommodate his pre-tournament news conference. It had to be held in a special hospitality tent.

When the tall, modest Martin entered the tent and saw the long row of television cameras and the crowd of reporters with notepads, he was taken aback.

"Wow," mouthed Martin, who took a seat behind a long table covered with a white tablecloth. "It's a bit overwhelming. I never could have dreamed that anything like this could have happened. It's like I'm a celebrity now. It's like I'm standing for something that's far greater than myself. The world is kind of watching to find out how I'm going to do with all this attention, and find out if I'm any good, really."

It didn't take the media throng long to discover that "the guy in the cart" can play this game a little. With the media in tow, he tore up the front nine of the difficult Jack Nicklaus-designed course with a five-under-par 31. His assault began

No, this isn't a putt to win the U.S. Open—it's just Casey being scrutinized by the media watchdogs at the 1998 Nike Tour's Greater Austin Open in Texas. (Chris Pietsch/the *Register-Guard*)

on the par-four third when he rolled in a twenty-five-foot putt for birdie. He followed that with another birdie on the par-four sixth. Then, on the 505-yard par-five eighth, Martin nailed a three-iron 245 yards on his second shot, leaving himself pin-high thirteen feet from the hole. He drained the putt for an eagle 3. Another birdie on the ninth left him at five under. He should have birdied the tenth but missed an easy six-footer.

After showing his talent and ability to score on the front, he proved his grit on the back. Poor chip shots on the fourteenth and sixteenth holes resulted in bogeys, and he was looking at another on the par-five eighteenth after getting stuck in trees on both sides of the fairway. But he sank a fifteen-footer from the back fringe to save par and shoot 69. It was quite a performance, given all the pressure. "Unreal," Mark Parry, a friend of Martin's, told the *Register-Guard,* Martin's hometown paper in Eugene, Oregon. Parry met Martin six years ago through the College Golf Fellowship, a religious organization. "I don't think Casey could have dreamed it up any better for his first round after the trial."

Robin Freeman, one of Martin's two playing partners that day, was impressed, if not filled with empathy. "He doesn't have any weaknesses," said Freeman, a veteran pro who has played on the regular tour. "He drives it long and pretty straight. He hits good iron shots; he can work the ball both ways. He's got a good putting touch. He's really a terrific kid. He's upbeat, outgoing, and he's got a lot to offer the Nike Tour, and he's got a lot to offer the PGA Tour when he gets up there. I have to admire his courage in order to fulfill his dream, to challenge the tour. But I also think the tour has the right to make its own rules."

Martin carefully crosses a stream in a ravine at the Greater Austin Open, near where an errant shot of his had ended up. Keep in mind, one misstep for Martin could mean a broken right leg and likely amputation. (Chris Pietsch/the *Register-Guard*)

All week long his exploits were front-page news back home. "Casey Martin to ride into golf history today," trumpeted the *Register-Guard,* and, "Austin golf gallery turning into Casey's Crowd."

Meanwhile, at Eugene Country Club, where Martin grew up playing and where his dad, King, plays weekly, members followed Casey's every move. After Martin pulled his drive on the eighteenth into a ravine during the second round, they became especially concerned, not so much for his score but for his bad leg, which is very brittle. A break could very well mean amputation. His ball came to rest on a small grassy split of land, less than ten yards wide, in the middle of a creek. Luckily for him, he could play the shot, and he hit a sand wedge back into the fairway. He then made a short leap back over the creek, coming down hard on his right leg and clearly wincing in pain. "I cringed when I saw that," says ECC member Don Gott.

Martin ended up with another 69, leaving him tied for eighth, three shots off the lead. He followed with an even-par 72 in the third round and, in bitterly cold weather, a final-round 78. Martin described it as the worst weather he's ever encountered in competitive play. Riding in the cart, ironically, only made the freezing temperatures worse. (His caddie, former Stanford golf teammate Steve Burdick, even suggested he walk.) His even-par score of 288 left him tied for sixteenth and was worth $3,031.

More valuable than the money was the respect Martin earned from those in the gallery witnessing the exploits of a young man determined to live out his dream. He was a living example of the PGA Tour's slogan "Anything's Possible." Among the thousands of spectators was nine-year-old Kern Loest, who followed Martin around during Friday's round on the shoulders of his father, Craig. Martin is Loest's Michael Jordan. A third-grader from Fort Worth, Loest suffers from a disorder almost the same as Martin's—Klippel-Trenaunay-Weber syndrome. It was the first time that either one had met another person with the rare problem. (There are only nine hundred reported cases worldwide.)

"There aren't many of us, are there?" Martin said to Kern, after autographing the boy's heavy support stocking, just like the one he wears. Martin also gave the young boy an autographed Nike cap and a Nike Tour T-shirt. Martin's newfound notoriety has given young Loest something else—an easy answer to the questions he hears all the time: "What's wrong with your leg?" or "Why do you limp?"

Who said using a golf cart gives a golfer an advantage over his fellow competitors? Martin's use of a golf cart actually put him at a disadvantage for the cold final round of the Greater Austin Open—he never got the chance to loosen up, even a little, that walking a course allows. (AP/Wide World photo by L. M. Otero)

Loest can now say, "Well, you know the golfer, Casey Martin? I've got what he has."

"He's really come out of his shell," says Kern's grandfather, Anton Loest. "It doesn't bother him as much as it once did. He has so much more confidence now. It's been a real blessing."

Before meeting Casey, Kern had never played golf, save for the miniature version. Now, he's teeing up at a local par-three course and has made a huge improvement in his physical therapy. "It gives him a goal to work on," says his mom, Karen. "Golf gives him an incentive. At nine years old, 'no pain, no gain' doesn't work. You can't tell him, 'If you don't work hard, you are not going to be able to walk when you are twenty.' Well, twenty seems very far away when you are nine. We now say, 'You keep working on this, you can keep playing golf.' It is immediate."

A month after Loest's family met Martin in Austin, they drove a couple hundred miles to see him again at the Nike Tour stop in Shreveport, Louisiana. "Casey is a super guy, too," Craig says. "He is the type of person we would love our son to look up to."

"ADVERSITY CAUSES
SOME MEN TO BREAK;
OTHERS TO BREAK RECORDS."

—William A. Ward

CHAPTER ONE

A Cross to Bear

Best known as home of the University of Oregon, Eugene is a bucolic burg two hours south of Portland, in the western part of the state. The town, named after explorer Eugene F. Skinner, who settled it in 1846, lies at the confluence of two pristine rivers, the mountain-fed McKenzie and the larger Willamette. Despite its rural location and the fact that the population (120,000) is overwhelmingly white (93 percent), Eugene is nevertheless a progressive, liberal city with cultural and social offerings impressive for a city its size. Annual events include the Oregon Bach Festival. Forty-nine parks encompass two thousand acres. As far as Casey Martin is concerned, the prettiest sight of all probably is the big contemporary-style concrete federal courthouse situated in the heart of downtown.

Eugene's growth rate in the nineties has outpaced the rest of the country because of three simple words: quality of life. Although the city has become big enough—the downtown streets are now one-way—people still don't worry about locking their doors at night. It retains a distinctive small-town feel. Most residents are careful to recycle, and they exercise in the piney, mountainous surroundings—when it's not raining, that is. The average rainfall is forty-three inches a year, and locals like to joke, "We don't tan, we rust." It rarely snows, however, and the climate is mild enough to play golf year-round. Indeed, the state has produced its share of touring professional golfers, such as Bob Gilder, Peter Jacobsen, and Eugene's own Brian Henninger.

Then, of course, there's Casey Martin. The younger of two boys, Casey was born on June 2, 1972. His dad, King, is a senior vice president with Smith Barney. His mom, Melinda, has dedicated her life to raising a family and charity work (she spends one day a week at the Pearl Buck Center, a nonprofit organization that provides services to the developmentally disabled). Melinda grew up in the Portland area. King is a native Eugenian. They met while attending the University of Oregon, where Melinda belonged to Pi Beta Phi and King was a member of Sigma Alpha Epsilon (he was the "yell king," the guy with the megaphone who leads the cheers at football games). They married in 1966 before their senior year of college and never left Eugene. Longtime season ticket holders to Duck sporting events, they never lost their school spirit. Family fun usually meant attending a football or basketball game. Well-liked by everyone, they're solid, pillar-of-the-community people and devout Baptists.

King and Melinda Martin are models of consistency in at least one respect: They have lived practically their entire married life in the same one-story home on Spring Boulevard in Eugene's South Hills, in the higher end of town, both figuratively and literally. An exclusive area, South Hills towers over the rest of Eugene. The homes, nestled in among tall pine trees, come with the best views and scenery in town.

The Martins' idyllic existence was shaken soon after Casey was born. Something, definitely, was wrong with Casey, and years would go by before anyone knew the extent of his problem. The infant's crying filled the house, especially at night, when he'd wake up wailing in pain. Casey's persistent crying couldn't be explained away simply as "colic." Something more serious was amiss, and it wasn't going away anytime soon. On sight, there didn't seem to be anything physically wrong with him.

"It was extremely difficult for King and Melinda, knowing their child was suffering and feeling helpless," says close family friend Bobbie Teague. "To have him screaming and crying

Casey Martin's childhood home in the exclusive South Hills area of Eugene, Oregon. (Photo by Tom Cunneff)

27

out in pain was such a worry. Many times they would rush him to the hospital emergency room when they couldn't comfort him during the night."

Perhaps the worst part was the mystery of it all. The Martins weren't even sure where the pain was coming from, and they hadn't made a connection between his suffering and the unusual port-wine birthmark on his right leg. It wasn't until they switched pediatricians just before Casey's first birthday that they became certain the problem was with his leg. "All told, they had four doctors working with Casey before his condition was finally diagnosed," Teague says.

One day in 1975 King happened to be playing golf with a doctor from an orthopedic clinic in Eugene, when he expressed his anxiety over Casey's condition. The doctor suggested he bring the boy in for a checkup. The Martins finally started to get some concrete answers, but it wasn't until Casey was five when they got a firm diagnosis: Their younger son was suffering a rare birth defect called Klippel-Trenaunay-Weber syndrome. Basically, the valves in the venal system of his right leg were faulty. Blood in a healthy leg is carried to the lower leg by arteries, and then pumped back up the leg through the veins. Because the blood is flowing up through the veins against gravity, valves in the vein are designed to prevent blood from draining back down. In the case of Casey's right leg, however, those vein valves never close. The blood never flows back up and out; instead, it pools in the lower part of the leg. The swelling is not only rapid and extremely painful, it can also lead to the deterioration of the leg and joints. Time and again, young Casey was required to have collections of blood removed from his knee with a syringe, followed by splinting and resting the leg.

King and Melinda were relieved to know that their son's condition had finally been properly diagnosed, although that knowledge did little to lessen Casey's obvious discomfort. "From the time he was a baby, he has lived with pain," Melinda told *Sports Illustrated*. "He used to hemorrhage every few months, and each time, we had to splint or put the leg in a cast." Following the diagnosis, doctors fitted Casey with a special stocking to help keep the blood circulating. (He now wears two hip-to-ankle rubberized Jobst stockings twenty-four hours a day; they come off only for showers.) "This gave Casey some measure of relief, but he was never completely pain-free," Teague says.

The birth defect, pronounced KLIP-pell Tre-NOW-nay VAY-bur, gets its name from the researchers who first described it in 1900. So few people have KTW, there aren't many, if any, doctors who specialize in it. Such a specialist probably couldn't make a living treating people with the disease. Treatment is difficult to come by, and the cause is elusive. One medical hypothesis is that the venous system in KTW victims suffered some sort of trauma during fetal development, or it could be genetic with a vague familial link—a great uncle, for example, with varicose veins.

One of the disease's few experts, Dr. David Driscoll, a pediatric cardiologist with the Mayo Clinic in Rochester, Minnesota, recently co-authored a paper on the management of 252 patients with KTW over a period of thirty-eight years. "The major frustration I've seen with patients is trying to find physicians who have seen enough cases, or *any* cases, to be able to offer any meaningful advice or direction," says Driscoll, who's now involved in a study to see if a gene defect is the cause. "That doesn't necessarily mean the parents passed on a gene defect to their child. It just means that during early development of the fetus, an abnormality occurs spontaneously and without explanation.

"All of us have a fifth finger that is shorter than our fourth finger. Why is that? How does that fifth finger know when to stop growing? It's because the receptors for a variety of growth factors know when to turn themselves off. If the receptors don't turn themselves on and off appropriately, you could get abnormal growth of blood vessels, abnormal growth of tissue, abnormal growth of everything. That is my speculation, but we can't prove it. That's what we are looking for right now. We are looking for that defect."

The odds of contracting the disease? Infinitely tiny. Furthermore, the syndrome also varies from person to person, making it difficult for doctors to properly treat and track. And while it usually affects the limbs, it can also attack the trunk, buttocks, or even the face. "It is really scary when something dramatic happens to your child and you realize that oftentimes you know more than the doctors," says Judy Vessey, who runs a KTW support group that has 550 members. Her seventeen-year-old daughter has KTW in her left leg. "Another problem is that it can be very physically disfiguring. Casey happens to be a really handsome kid. When he has pants on, you don't notice that he has something wrong with his leg. But a lot of these people have a port-wine stain covering half their body. It can be on their face, their arms; sometimes their legs can be twice as big as normal. I know kids who have never gotten into a bathing suit because they are so humiliated."

Imagine showing up at an HMO with this problem and finding out no one there has a clue. And the Mayo Clinic is not exactly on most people's managed-care list. But the publicity

Casey's plight has received is helping (the Martins themselves have been inundated with calls). "It certainly has brought a lot more people to the support group, which I think has helped the networking," Vessey says.

Even without a support group for Casey and his parents in those early days, they tried to make the best of the faith-testing situation. "They just accepted it, and they thrived on Casey's energy and willpower," says Coby McDonald, a close childhood friend. "It stopped being thought of as a negative early on, because Casey would never let it be a negative. And he will never let it be a negative."

Casey's situation was all the more poignant considering that the Martins are a very athletically minded family. He's a natural athlete who loves playing sports. Casey's favorite as a youth was basketball, which he often played on the court in the family's backyard. He is extremely close to his equally sporting brother, Cameron, Casey's senior by two years. Cameron Martin played varsity basketball at South Eugene High School before going on to the University of Oregon on a golf scholarship.

Casey's disability couldn't stop him from participating in a variety of physical activities, let alone sports, with his peers. When the kids on the block played football, he was the designated quarterback for both sides. After learning to kick with his left foot, he was the goalie on the soccer team. "He was an awesome goalie," says Austin Teague, who grew up with Casey and was a golfing teammate of his at South Eugene. "He was a brick wall."

Casey never complained. He never discussed his leg, even with his closest confidante, his brother. "I'm not an expert on chronic pain," Cameron told *Golf Digest,* "but I think that was his mechanism for staving it off. He never talked about it. He just limped home from the soccer games and iced his leg." New friends didn't learn about his condition unless the situation warranted. Not long after McDonald first met Casey in Mr. Debrick's math class at Roosevelt Middle School, he playfully slapped Casey on his right leg with the back of his hand. It wasn't a hard hit by any means, but Casey cringed. "I remember him wincing and looking at me," McDonald says. "I said, 'Oh, I'm sorry, do you have a bruise there?' And he said, 'No, I have this problem.' "

Martin, along with another friend, Joel Rubenstein, who grew up down the block from Casey, explained the problem to McDonald. "Casey was never the kind of guy who's like 'woe is me,' feeling sorry for himself," Rubenstein says. "It was never, 'Why am I like this? How come I can't play football with you guys all the time? Why do I have to sit down? Why is my leg hurting?'

"But growing up, it was all about sports, and I remember Casey sitting out sometimes, being careful."

Martin hated drawing attention to himself or his predicament. During "half-days" at Roosevelt, Casey, Rubenstein, and McDonald would hang out after school with a group of friends at a bowling alley or go for burgers. Kids from the other middle school frequently met up with them.

"I remember once where one of the guys from the other school bumped into him or something, and he kind of winced," McDonald recalls. "One of the girls said, 'You gotta watch out for his leg.' Casey just looked over at this girl and he didn't say anything. It wasn't other people's job. He didn't want other people to look out for him that way.

"He tried to avoid deep conversations about his leg with almost everybody. He knew that we knew what was going on, and he did not want our pity. Every now and again I would say something to him like, 'Is it all right?' He would always say it was fine. He didn't want to make it an issue."

Most of the other kids at his middle school weren't even aware how serious his problem was—even his first girlfriend, Sadie Ungemach. "He asked me to 'go' with him in the sixth grade, but it was a short-lived romance," she says. "He just came up to me in the hallway and asked me if I'd go with him. He just kind of blushed, and then he walked away. I don't think we talked for a week afterwards."

Never did she see him as crippled or disabled. "I remember Coby [McDonald] saying he's got this circulation problem and that's why he kind of limps a little bit. But it never even was an issue. I never thought about it until recently with all the media coverage. I didn't even know it was a painful experience for him or that it was something he really had to overcome. To me, he was fine the way he was. I had no idea.

"What's interesting is this girl we grew up with—her foot is kind of handicapped. But she really seemed handicapped to me. Her inner self-confidence and security in herself weren't there, so the fact that she was handicapped really crippled her whole life. She dropped out of high school and went the total opposite direction that Casey did."

Casey was someone Ungemach always admired and looked up to. It wasn't just that he was a great student, or that he once serenaded her at his house by playing Chicago's "You're the Inspiration" on the piano ("I was so impressed," she says). He was funny, too. One time in Mrs. Brown's "Sex and Stuff" class in the eighth grade, he and Joel Rubenstein had Sadie, the teacher, and all the other students in stitches as they pretended to be sperm racing for the egg during a class skit session.

33

"They had Mrs. Brown rolling. She had tears running down her face, she was laughing so hard," Ungemach says. "It was very funny. It was really fun taking classes with him. He was a good role model for me in a way. In all my classes, he was the one who spoke up and was the teacher's favorite."

Like most any kid, Casey just wanted to be normal, or at least perceived that way. And to a large extent he was. Up until the eighth grade, he played almost every sport the other kids did. His leg hadn't deteriorated enough yet.

But there were moments where exceptions had to be made. On Halloween, for example. "When we were eight or ten years old and went trick-or-treating in his neighborhood, we would have to stop back at his house after one round," Teague says. "It got painful walking up and down those hills, and he would prop up his leg for about an hour before we could go out again."

Then there were times when the local kids would play "Rambo" in the surrounding forest. "It was tough for him not being part of the neighborhood gang all the time," says Scott Houmes, a friend of Cameron's. "We were running around doing our own thing, and we were so young we didn't understand his condition. He was odd man out at times. But he was a great athlete. He did very well compared to what you'd think. His parents might have held him back, but for good reason. They probably understood his condition better than we did."

While the other players on the Roosevelt Middle School basketball team would do wind sprints, Casey would be off to the side doing push-ups. His leg couldn't take running. "He wouldn't just stand there and watch," McDonald says.

Casey's close friends became educated early on about his condition. Their instructions were not to roughhouse too much with him and to avoid bumping his right leg. "It wasn't like when you were playing basketball you couldn't touch him or guard him or anything like that," says Teague, who would sometimes help him put on his stocking. "It was just be aware, be cautious."

Casey spent a lot of time alternately icing his leg or soaking in the Jacuzzi at his house. His friends rarely saw his leg because he wore his Jobst stocking all the time, even in the hot tub. McDonald recalls a time or two when Martin was getting the stocking repaired and got into the Jacuzzi without it.

"He was very sensitive about it, even in front of me," McDonald says. "His leg is not a pretty thing to see. It is amazingly thin. It is just the bone and then it's purple. The whole thing looked like a really, really old woman's. You see all the veins and where the blood goes. It didn't bother me. I wasn't gawking at it, but if you are not sensitive about [his] feelings, you could easily hurt him."

There wasn't one dramatic moment when Casey's sporting life, save for golf, ended. "It was an educated decision he and his family had to make as far as his future was concerned," Teague says. "Golf was his main interest and, the way things were going with the steady deterioration of his leg, his chances for playing college and professional golf could have been eliminated."

Beginning in the eighth grade, Casey limited team-sport activities to tossing the football or games of H-O-R-S-E: he was the neighborhood champ. "Oh, he was phenomenal," Teague says. "He could light it up from anywhere."

Martin focused his life on four areas: school, Bible study, piano, and golf. He could light it up from anywhere in those, too.

CHAPTER TWO

A Game He Could Play

When it came to golf, Casey was on equal footing, if not equal legs, with everyone else. He started playing when he was six, introduced to the game by his father. King is a ten-handicapper who joined Eugene Country Club in 1976. The non-equity club, established in 1899, is situated just north of downtown across the Willamette River. It has about 550 members and costs thirty-five thousand dollars to join—pretty pricey for the area but well worth it, given it has one of the best courses in the state.

ECC's Robert Trent Jones course measures 6,854 yards from the back tees, but it plays longer. There's not a lot of roll due to the often-soggy conditions. The holes, bordered by huge eighty-foot Douglas firs, are tight. They curve both right and left, so players have to work the ball both ways to score well. Water comes into play on many of the holes, and the greens are fast and undulating. Champions grow in this sort of fertile field. It's easy to see why ECC has produced so many fine golfers like Casey, his fellow Nike tourist Eric Johnson, and Brian Henninger. "He doesn't get surprised anywhere, having played here," says ECC head pro Ron Weber.

Young Casey literally grew up at the club, and his irregular gait became as familiar a sight as three-putts on the tricky greens. "He always limped around," longtime member Don Gott says. "After a while, you just didn't pay any attention. You always saw him with that stocking on. He never complained or said a word about his leg."

Fortunately for Casey, his problem was with his right leg, not the left. Had it been the other way around, he'd never have become the golfer he has. For a right-handed golfer like Casey, the left leg supports a great deal of weight transfer during the downswing and on through to the follow-through. His right leg would not be able to withstand such stress.

"Well, it would have been a problem," says Al Mundle, head pro at ECC from 1981 to 1984 and one of Casey's two instructors to this day (the other is Doral's renowned Jim McLean). "I don't know that he could have played right-handed. He probably would have had to play left-handed had it been his other leg."

When he first started playing golf, Casey's game didn't stand out as exceptional. Because of his leg, however, he was getting lessons in the most important part of the game—inner fortitude—long before anyone else his age was. Mundle can remember a number of times that an exhausted, slump-shouldered Martin would come off the course mid-round, tears streaming down his cheeks.

"Casey, what's wrong?" he'd ask, but Martin wouldn't answer at first. He just bit his lip and shook his head. "Are you

Eugene Country Club and its Robert Trent Jones–designed golf course was like a second home to Casey. (Photo by Tom Cunneff)

sure you're okay?" Mundle said. "Is there anything I can help you with?"

Casey straightened up his shoulders, wiped the tears off his face, and said, "No sir, Mr. Mundle, I'm just fine."

"Then he went home," Mundle recalls. "But he was in such terrible pain. Most of the time he could make it through okay. He would just hobble around. But he did not want any sympathy from anybody. He did not want any special favors. He just took what he had, and he was going to make the best of it. And that's the way he has been in life. It has made him a very strong individual and a wonderful person."

Martin never discussed his leg with Mundle, even during lessons on the large range at ECC, just to the left of the first hole. But Mundle took into consideration the fact that Martin can't make a full weight shift onto the right side in his backswing. Ironically, it probably helped him develop a better swing, not unlike that of his future Stanford teammate, Tiger Woods.

"I don't feel it really affected his swing that much," Mundle says. "He has been able to work the swing in spite of it. He does what a lot of players work hard to do, which is restrict the lower body turn and create torque. That's the key to hitting the ball a long way—creating torque. He tends to stay a little bit left of center. He has a wonderful turnback. He's also big and long-armed, and extremely flexible."

Casey often played golf with Cameron, or Cam, as he's known, who was more than happy to have his little brother tagging along. Cam was quietly but fiercely protective of Casey. The two slept in adjacent bedrooms with their beds pushed up against opposite sides of the same wall, and Cam would often be awakened during the night by Casey's crying on the other side. As they got older, Casey no longer cried, but he would moan and thrash his way through a fitful night's sleep, getting up many times to elevate his leg. Unlike many sibling relationships, Cam was more reassuring than competitive to Casey during their rounds together. If Casey was struggling with his swing, Cam would help him straighten it out on the range, and vice versa. Like a cyclist, Casey drafted off Cam's talent and support.

"Cam was very determined," Mundle says. "If he was forty yards away and he had to get it up and down in two, that's what he would do. He's gutsy." Casey was the same way. "When you saw him on the tee, you could see the determination there. You don't see that in a lot of kids at that age. He was focused. It's like Ben Hogan after his accident. He came back stronger than ever. And you see that time after time after time."

Casey and Cam had outstanding junior careers. Melinda was the long-distance-driving "soccer mom." From the southern Oregon town of Medford and the Rogue Valley Country Club, over to the coast at Coos (Bay) Country Club, and up north to Portland's Riverside Golf and Country Club, she ferried her two boys and usually a friend or two to junior events.

Because of his sensitive leg, Casey really couldn't share a bed. When his leg started to throb in the middle of the night, he'd get up and lie with his back on the floor and stick his leg up the wall to drain the blood out of it. But he always walked the next day at the tournament and carried his bag, remembers childhood friend D. J. Quinney, who toured often with him. "He was top-three in every tournament we played," he says. "I mean, there wasn't a tournament where he had a bad round. You knew his time would come."

Casey ended up with seventeen junior titles. His first state victory came in the second flight of the PeeWee Division (ages eight to eleven), at Tualatin Country Club near Portland, right around the time of his tenth birthday. But that summer, Casey's leg took a notable turn for the worse. Until that time, pain didn't develop in his leg, particularly his knee, until several hours or days after physical activity. With rest, the discomfort would disappear. Now, however, the aches began just ten to fifteen minutes later and would last much longer. So on August 16, 1982, Casey had the first of four corrective arthroscopic knee surgeries. The internal bleeding had already begun to take its toll. The operation revealed extensive inflammation and considerable roughening of the back of the kneecap.

"The first arthroscopy was quite beneficial," his orthopedic surgeon, Dr. Donald Jones, testified at the 1998 trial. "Although it did not totally resolve Casey's knee pain, it certainly improved his comfort level."

In December 1986, at age fourteen, Casey had a second arthroscopy. Unfortunately, the benefits were only short-term. If the leg wasn't in good working order, at least his heart was. The trophies that cluttered his room were testimony to that. In the summer of 1986, Martin was the youngest in the nation to qualify for the Big I Insurance Youth Golf Classic in Springfield, Ohio. (He missed the cut in the seventy-two-hole event.) The following year, he edged his older brother in a play-off at the sectionals for a second consecutive trip to the Big I Insurance Youth Golf Classic. He wound up finishing eighteenth at the national tournament, in Pinehurst, North Carolina.

Later in that summer of 1987, he and Cam represented the state in the Hogan Cup Team Matches. The prestigious event pits the top five juniors from seven Western states and British Columbia in a two-day, medal-play tournament in Oregon. An article in the *Register-Guard* previewing the Martin boys' participation in the Hogan Cup said that "one of the major concerns about Casey has been his stamina. His veins were not formed correctly from the knee down in his right leg at birth, and his knee often swells from internal bleeding.... In a tournament, the condition can plague him."

"It does bother me when I shift my weight," said Casey, who finished tied for nineteenth out of forty-five (Cam came in seventh). "I had a lesson, and learned how to rearrange it [his weight]. I just try not to let it bother me."

Whatever he had done, the story noted, it worked. He won six tournaments in his 14-15 age group, and he was the only 14-15-year-old to qualify for the Hogan Cup that summer. Despite his leg disability, Casey always walked, even hilly courses like those at Grants Pass and Coos (Bay) Country Clubs, which were always more painful for him. He had to quit playing on only a couple of occasions, like the time during the high school district championships his freshman year at South Eugene. The district and state championships were always harder on Casey because they were two-day, thirty-six-hole events, while the matches during the regular season were one-day tournaments. When he should be resting his leg, he would go out and walk another eighteen holes.

After struggling to an atrocious 87 on the opening day of the districts at Tokatee Golf Course, he had to quit after two holes the following day. While South Eugene as a team didn't do well, Cam finished second in the individual standings (he won the tournament the year before) and then went on to claim the state high school title a week later. His exploits were front-page news in the *Register-Guard's* sports section and the beginning of an extraordinary amount of local press accorded the Martins, especially Casey.

"I think it was definitely a problem. Our team was upset about it," says Kit Wilbur, who played against the Martin brothers when he attended Churchill High School, where he's now the coach. "I almost feel bad about being upset. Casey was really a pretty cool kid. He was not a braggart at all. He just wanted to play. The whole leg thing wasn't a real big issue. I never heard Casey talk about it. Obviously, it was a big deal, but for most of the kids playing with him, we were aware of it, but it wasn't an issue. It wasn't, 'Oh God, I wonder if Casey is going to be able to withstand all eighteen holes,' or, 'Is he going to collapse?' It wasn't that at all. The issue was who'd play the best golf that day, and it was usually Casey."

To the local press, however, "Martin limps to victory" was an irresistible angle. He received a fair amount of press training, something that would come in handy later on. "He is used to being a semipublic figure," says childhood friend Rubenstein. "He was always on the local news. He was comfortable. He wasn't ashamed or embarrassed at all having people pay attention to him. That shows now in how well he handles himself under the press of media."

Claiming the state high school title was one of the highlights of Cam's career, and he did it in dramatic fashion. Playing in the penultimate group on the final day at Glendoveer Golf Course in Portland, Cam, then a junior, posted a one-under-par score for the thirty-six-hole event. He was sitting at the scorer's table thinking he would, at best, finish as co-champion. His closest competitor, Terry Blake of

Centennial High School, was tied with Cam as he stood over his ball on the final green. A three-putt, however, left Cam as the sole champion. He was right back in the thick of the hunt for the state title the following year. The guy he had to beat? His brother Casey.

CHAPTER THREE

Straight Shooter

The turning point in Casey's golf game came his sopho-more year in high school. With Cam in his senior year, the South Eugene Axemen (so named for local loggers) were the golf team to beat in the county, if not the state. Led by the Martin brothers, they won five of their eight regular-season events, beating an average of ten other high schools each time in four-man aggregate eighteen-hole, stroke-play competitions.

South Eugene was the heavy favorite going into the district championships. The front page of the *Register-Guard's* sports section pictured Cam and Casey standing with a set of clubs, headlined "Martin Brothers Set to Take a Swing at 5AAA Golf Title." With his season stroke average close to 73, Cam, the article noted, was the individual favorite. Casey, who had a stroke average closer to 76, "has one of the finest short games in the state." His coach attributed this to the fact he couldn't play as many rounds as the others, so he spent a lot of time chipping and putting.

The article recounted "horror stories" of their first district tournaments their respective freshman years, when Cam shot an 89 the second day and Casey had to withdraw because of his leg. It also noted that, although coaches agreed to let Casey use a cart, he did so only once during the season. That was at a tournament in Grants Pass in Southern Oregon when he and an opponent, Cam Mitchell of Sheldon High School, who had been undergoing radiation treatment for Hodgkin's disease, shared a cart. "We normally prefer to walk," Casey said.

Under difficult weather conditions in the first round of the districts, South Eugene took the lead over Sheldon by five shots and Churchill High School by seventeen. True to their

South Eugene High School, home to the Axemen and where Casey and Cam Martin excelled as golfers. (Photo by Tom Cunneff)

season averages, Cam shot a 73, while Casey turned in a 77. On the second day, however, Sheldon swept past South Eugene for the championship when three of its players shot in the 70s, while Cam and Casey faltered, shooting 81 and 79, respectively. The two teams advanced to the state finals the following week, and Casey and Cam qualified for state individual honors as well—they finished in the top five.

"I always remember Casey being very positive, very enthusiastic, and very talented," says Gerry Norquist, who was the coach of Sheldon then. "Casey was physically growing a lot. He was a pretty tall kid. I remember there were times when you could tell he was in a little more pain than other times, but he never used a cart for an extended period."

Norquist is a former assistant pro at Eugene Country Club and a close friend of Casey's who testified on his behalf at the trial. He first met a flagpole-thin, bespectacled Martin when he was about thirteen. The two have since played many rounds together. "I knew he had some ability. He still hadn't grown into his body but was able to launch 270-yard drives," says Norquist, who now plays on the Asian tour. "There were times, even back then, when you could tell Casey's good days and bad days. He had more of a noticeable limp. There were times when you'd think, maybe he just shouldn't be out there if he was hurting that much. I don't remember him ever walking off."

In the late eighties, when Norquist was at ECC, the board granted Casey a special exemption that permanently waived the cart fee. Martin rarely took advantage of it. "We always walked," says Norquist, who got to see just what Casey's problem was one summer's day in the bag room after a round. "He told me it was hurting. I was curious about his leg. He didn't make a grand production out of it. He said, 'I don't like to show it much. It's kind of ugly.' He rolled his stocking down, and for the first time I could see what he was dealing with. It was ghastly. It wasn't a nice sight. It was like a bouquet of flowers. It was yellow, blue, green, everything. It looked like a very bad bruise. I remember in college I got kicked in the leg and got a big bruise and missed a week of golf. The blood drained down into my foot and I thought, 'My God, they're going to have to amputate it.' It reminded me of that. That was ten or twelve years ago [when he saw the leg], and there's no way his situation has gotten any better."

After losing to Sheldon in the districts, South Eugene got their revenge at the AAA state high school boys championship at Glendoveer Golf Course in Portland. Casey tied for the first-round lead with a 72, while Cam opened the defense of his title with a 75, helping South take the team lead. The next day, the Martin boys shot matching 75s to lead South Eugene to a first-place finish over fifteen teams. It was the school's first state title in history. Casey lost out on the individual honors by one shot, while Cam finished third. Commented Cam in the school yearbook, "It was a rewarding way to end my high school career. Last year I won the state individual title and this year, with my younger brother, our team won the state title. I couldn't have asked for anything more."

While Cam was off on a golf scholarship at the University of Nevada at Las Vegas, where he played No. 3, Casey took his game and his team to a new level his junior year. With a stroke average of 73, he led the Axemen to six wins in the seven regular-season tournaments of 1989, and then a first-place finish in the district championships. Shooting rounds of 71 and 72, Casey also won the medalist honors by eight strokes. His one-under-par total of 143 broke the nine-year-old district record of 144 that was held by Eric Johnson, Casey's fellow Nike tourist. "What was amazing was that he went out and made it look so easy," Eric's father, Steve Johnson, the Churchill High coach, told the *Register-Guard.* "There was no fanfare. It just showed me how good he is."

"They say the good ones—the Mickey Mantles and the Magic Johnsons—make it look easy, and that's exactly what Casey's doing," reporter Dave Kayfes wrote. "And, what's most remarkable in his case, he's doing it with one bad leg."

"Golf is the one sport I can do. It forces me to forget the pain. It's given me the determination and work ethic to overcome," said Martin, who had picked up some added distance off the tee since the previous season, cranking it 260 yards or farther. "I've grown a couple of inches. As a result, I'm getting more lash and hitting the ball longer."

His best was yet to come. At the state championships, Casey was tied for fifth after a first-round, even-par 72 at Glendoveer. When his three teammates all shot in the mid-70s, South dipped under 300 strokes for the first time in the school's history and took the first-round lead. The team was poised to become the first school from their district to win back-to-back titles in thirty-five years. "This was the best day ever for a South Eugene golf team," said South's late golf coach, Al Fletcher. "The conditions were ideal, and everyone played brilliantly."

With high winds, the weather was less than ideal the next day. Martin persevered through the difficult conditions, matching his one-under-par total of 143 at the districts to take medalist honors. He trailed by a shot as he made the turn, then shot two under on the final nine to win by two shots. Casey

The South Eugene High School golf team shown in the 1988 yearbook included both Cam Martin, a senior (second from left), and Casey Martin, a sophomore (fourth from left). They flank coach Al Fletcher. (Photo courtesy of South Eugene High School)

played with considerable pain, especially on the second day. "What he did was unreal," Fletcher said. "We were playing in thirty- to forty-mile-per-hour winds and to go two under on the back side was an unbelievable display of golf." Said Martin, "I didn't hit the ball well today at all. Finally, somehow, I was able to scramble and make pars." His outstanding performance wasn't enough, however, to help South claim the team title; they finished second by five shots.

"He was the favorite," Norquist remembers. "It seemed like every time we played, Casey was going to be a contender in every single tournament. He was that far above the field." And that far past the field in the fairway. "Casey is very long and he has a tremendously fundamental golf swing," Norquist adds. "I have always felt he has a really good touch around the greens. And I think this is very important: He comes from a family which has always stressed belief in yourself, in God, and in doing the right thing. That is going to help you feel good about yourself. That is important in the game of golf."

Casey had other reasons to feel good about himself in high school. "He is as well-rounded as they come," says childhood friend Rubenstein. "He certainly wasn't just about golf." Martin was a straight-A student who graduated first in his class with a 3.98 average (he had only two B's his entire four years!). He became an accomplished piano player after the family grabbed a white spinet from an aunt who decided to get rid of it. A room just off the kitchen became his private music sanctuary. With his right leg stretched out and his left foot working the pedals, he liked to play everything from Prince's "Purple Rain" to the theme from *Hill Street Blues* to classical. "I would be over there and Casey would start playing," Rubenstein remembers. "He was amazing."

Though modest by nature, Casey wasn't so humble that he wouldn't show off his musical ability once in a while. He would often play the piano inside the men's locker room at Eugene Country Club. Says member Neil Richards: "One day when I came in, somebody was playing. Hell, it was beautiful. It was some popular tune. I played with his dad that day and he said, 'That's Casey.' I didn't even know he could play."

At a friend's birthday party in high school, Martin displayed his talent. "He played a few songs on the piano and everybody was wowed, because most of the time people play chopsticks or fiddle around, and he got on there and started playing ragtime. Everybody was cheering for him," Austin Teague recalls. "No one ever thought he would be such a good piano player because he was so good at golf."

It's no surprise that a good-looking, multitalented guy like Martin was popular with the girls, even though he didn't have a steady, according to friends. Perhaps the girl who came closest was Lindsay Jones, the daughter of his doctor, who grew up

This South Eugene yearbook photo shows Casey in action as a junior in 1989, hitting shots at the Eugene Country Club's practice range. He went on to win the state high school golf title that year. (Photo courtesy of South Eugene High School)

down the block. They've remained close: She was there to cheer him on at his post-trial tournament in Austin. "Girls weren't a priority," Teague says. "It's not like he ever had a problem that way—he dated a few—but he just focused so much on golf and school."

Still, he managed to snag some pretty good prom dates. His junior year he took a six-foot-tall, blonde bombshell named Cici who left all the other guys drop-jawed. Senior year, he had two dates! He first asked his old friend Sadie Ungemach and then happily escorted Sadie's best friend, Mindy Codding, when she ended up dateless. The guy had good taste. While most high school kids show up in something like a powder-blue tux, Martin had the good sense to wear a classic black one.

Naturally, he picked them both up in a limo and gave them corsages. He never turned down a dance, even with his leg. "He's a great dancer," Ungemach says. "I think he got kind of sweaty. He had to juggle us all night. It was tough."

Alas, there was no goodnight kiss, save for a chaste peck on the cheek. "I used to kiss him on the cheek all the time, and he'd always blush," Ungemach recalls. "That was the joke. Coby always made fun of him."

Sex was no laughing matter to Martin, however. He was saving himself for marriage. "He was clear about that all the way through high school," Ungemach says. "He wasn't going to have sex till marriage—him and his brother both. It was definitely odd. That was not the norm at all. We grew up really fast. We were pretty bad. Everyone was like, 'Casey, he's so innocent and conservative.' He was a solid rock, especially compared to all of us."

Unlike a lot of the other kids at South Eugene, Martin didn't experiment with sex and drugs. "Not at all," Ungemach says. "He was a good influence on me. I went through a lot in high school and he was always just solid for me. I knew I could tell him things, and I knew he would never pass judgment on me. He was always a true good friend. He definitely has a strong internal compass. He doesn't have control of his leg but maybe everything else in his life he needed to have good control over."

It was clear Casey knew how to have a good time. "For the first year or two in high school, he was a great partyer," Rubenstein says. "I think he kind of hit a point where he realized that it wasn't very important to him, going out and getting hammered. I think he had bigger plans at that point, something more important to do. I definitely remember him drinking, but I also remember when he stopped. He would still go out. He was not one to stay home and say, 'Woe is me.' He's not like that. He knows what people do in high school. He would always go out and be very sociable, but he didn't need any alcohol."

No doubt it had something to do with his deepening faith in Jesus Christ. The Martins have always been a very religious family and have belonged to First Baptist Church in downtown Eugene for fifteen years. "Casey's father tries to live like God would want him to live, according to biblical guidelines," says First Baptist's Rudy Herr, Casey's youth pastor. "I think one of Casey's heroes is his dad. He speaks highly of his father and they have a very good relationship."

"Casey talked about his parents all the time, and that isn't really cool in high school either, to talk about how great your parents are," Ungemach says. "I always wanted to be a part of their family. I feel like his sister in a lot of ways. They're just the perfect Beaver Cleaver family."

Casey had *two* dates for his senior prom. Longtime friend Sadie Ungemach is in the middle, and her friend Mindy Codding is on the left. (Photo courtesy of Sonja Snyder)

"The whole family is very religious, but they're not preachy," says Bruce Chase, a good friend of King Martin's and a fellow ECC member. "You'd never know they even belonged to a church." The only hint might be the silent prayer Casey would say over his meal in the grillroom at ECC after a round. "He's the only one who does it," says another member, Don Gott.

Unlike a lot of serious golfers, Casey's Sunday mornings weren't spent on the course, but at church. After services, he would attend the hour-and-a-quarter youth group meetings with students from other area high schools; he also was a regular at the one-hour Wednesday Bible study groups. "Even as a teenager, when teenagers can be rather childish and selfish, Casey was not that way," Herr says. "He had a maturity about him. He was quiet, but when he spoke, he spoke great words. He was a wise guy in a good sense of the word. He was looked up to by the one hundred-plus kids that attended this youth

Casey's senior picture (top row, fourth from left) showed him as photogenic as he was popular. Good buddy Coby McDonald is pictured in the bottom row, second from the left. (Photo courtesy of South Eugene High School)

group. Everyone knew how successful a golfer he was because it was in the papers, but you would never guess that by his demeanor. He was humble and kind. It wasn't like, 'Hey, here I am.' He was an unassuming guy. In other words, he was not untouchable like some people that are very successful."

There were times, however, when he could be a little overbearing with his less-than-devout friends. "I was not raised religiously and he accepted that with me, and he didn't try and convert me," Coby McDonald says. "But there were definitely times when … I like to go out and have a drink, and he used to go out with us even though he doesn't drink. But for a time, he even stopped doing that. I think it made him feel uncomfortable because there was definitely a transformation going on in him about really embracing God and religion. I think he is more comfortable with that now because he is more settled and at peace with it. I have seen other people go through that transformation as well, and as you're embracing and accepting it, there is that transition period where you cannot be around people who are not going through the same thing. He wanted other people to go through it as well. It was so spiritual and good for him that he wanted other people to see that as well."

Those are about the harshest words you'll ever hear about Casey—unless you're talking about his eating habits, which are pretty strange. He likes his food plain. For a while in childhood, he ate nothing but white rice. "I remember he was Mr. Plain, no fixings or anything," Rubenstein recalls. "He was the guy at McDonald's who orders no onions, no pickles, and it takes fifteen extra minutes. 'Hamburger plain, ketchup on the side.' He was really finicky. He would have a turkey sandwich with nothing on it, just bread—no mayonnaise, no tomato. He is a no-condiment kind of guy."

Martin's eating habits didn't seem to affect his growth any. By his senior year, he stood tall at six-foot-one and weighed 155 pounds. Although his right leg became more bothersome his final year at South Eugene, he managed to continue his outstanding play, leading the school to an undefeated regular season in 1990. Team members normally didn't play together, but there was one tournament that year at Tokatee Golf Club that was team match play. In a best-ball competition, Martin and the No. 2 player Teague were supposed to trounce their opponents from Thurston High School, but Teague didn't play well so it was much more tightly contested. Martin never gave up on him, however.

"Coming down the back nine, Casey gave me a lot of encouragement," Teague recalls. "I was struggling and he picked me up. I ended up finishing solid because he gave me so much encouragement and kept saying, 'Let's keep it together.' He is such a strong competitor. He hated to lose, but he wasn't a poor sport or anything. He had as good a sense of sportsmanship as anybody did, but he was very adamant about doing your best. He birdied three holes in a row and we ended up winning. He really turned it on, and his leg was really bothering him. He was limping pretty badly because he hit his knee getting out of a van. He was in a lot of pain. I knew he was in so much pain because I knew him so well, but most people would never know because he was adamant about not showing it at all.

"The competitive fire Casey has, I have never seen before, and I have played a lot of tournament golf, not just in high school. He is such a fierce competitor. Even with the distraction the pain caused, he stayed focused on what he had to do. That is what was so phenomenal. He didn't let the pain get to him. He could have called it quits and said, 'I can't play any-more, I can barely walk.' Instead, he turns around and birdies three holes in a row. He was amazing."

At the district championships that May, Martin actually relented and took a cart to finish his first round at Tokatee. (He later told his coach he had never played in so much pain.) Somehow he still played well enough to take the lead, shoot-ing a 76. "I felt a clicking feeling in my leg," he said. "On the eighth hole, it started getting real painful. Fortunately, the dis-trict let me take a cart." With Martin shooting a 78 the next day, the Axemen chopped their way to a second straight league title, and Martin successfully defended his district championship—barely. His one-stroke lead over Thurston's Andy Scheidt turned into a one-stroke deficit when he double-bogeyed the thirteenth hole. He made up the differ-ence when he birdied the par-three fifteenth. After they traded bogeys, Martin held on to win when he sank a four-foot putt on the last hole. Scheidt bogeyed.

"I am fortunate to get away with a win here because I didn't deserve it," said Martin, whose 154 total was eleven shots higher than his record score of the year before. "I putted so poorly, it was a joke. Usually under pressure I putt fine, but today for some reason I was a basket case." The leg hurt, but not enough to take a cart. "I put a wrap on it today so it wouldn't move very much. It hurt but it wasn't as bad as yes-terday. The real pain was my putting—I was pulling and push-ing everything right and left."

At the state championships a week later, he was offered the use of a cart but didn't take it, even though the Glendoveer Golf Course was very wet, which made walking difficult for everyone. In defense of his title, Martin opened the tournament with a 74 and a tie for second. "But there was some doubt whether he was going to play the second day of the two-day tournament," says Bryn Dearborn, another teammate. "After that round, his leg started to swell, and his mother didn't want him to play. Our hotel rooms were next to each other, and that was the discussion going on."

Nobody knew it though, because Martin, tired of people asking him questions about his leg, refused to say much about it. Battling to become only the fourth golfer to win back-to-back individual titles, a limping Martin held a one-shot lead on the second day over his playing partner, Brodie Berg of Reynolds High School, after making a birdie on the 515-yard, par-five fifteenth. But then he topped his drive on the seventeenth, another par-five, and made bogey to even the match. Martin and Berg went to the 277-yard, par-four finishing hole even. Berg drove five feet short of the green, while Martin's tee shot hit a tree, leaving a twenty-five-yard pitch. Martin, "aggressive as always," noted the *Register-Guard,* and knowing that Berg had a good chance of making birdie, hit his pitch twenty feet past the pin trying to get it close. After Berg chipped to tap-in range, Martin's putt for a tie slid five feet past the hole. As it turned out, a total of only two strokes were all that stood between Martin and what could have been three consecutive state titles. "It's been a helluva four years," his coach, Al Fletcher, said to him. "I've enjoyed it (more) than you did. It was a great try today; you didn't back away."

That summer Martin finished first in Oregon sectional qualifying for the prestigious U.S. Amateur, just as his brother Cam had the year before. In previewing his trip to the tournament at Denver's Cherry Hills and Meridian golf courses, Ron Bellamy, the *Register-Guard's* sports columnist, wrote presciently about Martin and his problematic limb. "The leg has shaped his past and looms over his future, and, of course, has an impact today. Put it this way: If not for his leg problem, Martin would be planning on becoming a professional golfer after college. He'd be setting that goal and all the intermediate goals leading up to it. But he doesn't know if the leg will hold up. If it is a choice between professional golf and being able to walk when he is forty—and, he said, it is not unrealistic to think he could face that choice—Casey Martin will choose to walk when he is forty."

There was no mention of the right to use a cart. At the U.S. Amateur, Martin shot rounds of 77-74 and failed to advance to match play. Shortly after that, he left for Stanford, where the specter of thirty-six-hole days, carrying his own bag, loomed on the horizon.

CHAPTER FOUR

A Bad Walk Spoiled

Stanford men's golf coach Wally Goodwin first met Martin in the summer of 1989 on a recruiting trip to San Diego for the Optimist Junior World championships. Martin played terrifically, shooting rounds of 75, 69, 75, and 72 on Torrey Pine's tough South Course, and he finished second. Goodwin was impressed with the way Martin kept his right knee bent and stable throughout the swing, something he usually had to teach his recruits. Only later did Goodwin learn that Martin kept his right leg bent all the time because of his disability, and that's when he knew that Casey was someone he wanted to have on his team. Indeed, he was his number-one choice that year.

"The heart is the premier thing with me, not golf ability," Goodwin told *People* magazine. Academics count with Goodwin, too. School parameters require him to recruit genuine student-athletes with a grade-point average of at least 3.6

(on a 4.0 scale) or SATs in the 1200 range. "What kind of kids are they internally—are they relentless? Casey's relentless."

Goodwin knows something about competitive heart, too, since his coaching career spans four decades in just about every sport imaginable. Many other golf coaches around the country wondered why Goodwin was going after Martin. "I sort of wondered to myself, so what were their thoughts, because I try to find youngsters who have a big, big heart," he testified at the trial. "And Casey had the biggest heart I'd ever seen."

University of Oregon golf coach Steve Nosler, likewise, tried to get Martin on his team, where he would have rejoined his brother, Cam, who had transferred over from University of Nevada at Las Vegas. But the academics and the better weather at Stanford, about an hour south of San Francisco, won out. He also needed to get away from home for a while, but it was a tough decision. Casey is a "Duck fan for life."

"I understood his decision as far as going to Stanford," says Nosler, who's also a longtime family friend (King worked for him part-time at his clothing store while in college). "Casey is a young man who goes after everything full bore."

Martin didn't disappoint, either on or off the course. He and Goodwin grew very close. During his freshman year, Martin sat Goodwin down one night in a motel while on the road and said, "Coach, listen, if you're going to have to put up with me for four or five years, I'm going to show you my leg." He removed his compressive stocking and his leg began to swell and become discolored. "I was glad that he—that he did that," Goodwin said at the trial. "But it was not my most enjoyable moment."

Martin and another new golf recruit, Notah Begay III, were cornerstones in Goodwin's rebuilding of the Cardinal golf team after he came to the school in the late eighties. "When Wally came in they were really struggling," says Sara Hallock, who played on the women's team before becoming Goodwin's administrative assistant (she now plays on the LPGA Tour). "He spent a lot of time trying to recruit some really good players. When Casey and Notah were freshmen, they really started to play a lot better. By the time they were sophomores, they were recognized as a really good team."

Hallock started at Stanford the same year as Martin and lived in the same freshman dorm in Wilbur Hall. She remembers him having a "weird" roommate from New York, but that didn't bother Martin. "Casey gets along with everybody," she says, adding that most people were unaware of his disability. "He was okay freshman year. He limped a little bit. Nobody even really noticed until he wore shorts. You'd be walking with him six months into the school year with someone who he knows and they'd say, 'Casey, why are you limping?' He would just look at them, totally deadpan, and say, 'I was born without a deep venous system.' They'd be like, 'Okay, whatever.'" End of conversation.

After his freshman year, when the team won one tournament and finished fifteenth at the NCAAs, Martin returned home to become the Pacific Northwest Amateur medalist and qualify for the 1991 U.S. Amateur to be played at the Honors Course in Ooltewah, Tennessee. Shooting a four-over-par 146 to qualify for match play, he extended defending champion Phil Mickelson to the nineteenth hole in the opening round. Strongly backed by the sizable gallery, Martin bowed out at the 401-yard nineteenth when Mickelson hit a wedge to two feet.

Martin got his revenge on Mickelson at the end of his sophomore year when he helped the Cardinal to the Pac-10

Conference title. They scored a stunning nineteen-stroke victory, upsetting Mickelson's heavily favored Arizona State team, as well as Arizona. Those two schools had been ranked No. 1 and No. 2 in the nation. The best part was that it happened in Martin's backyard, at the Trysting Tree Golf Club near Portland. "This is a great feeling," he told the *Oregonian*. "There's nothing like it." Stanford then went on to a ninth-place finish in the 1992 NCAA Championship, and Martin, who averaged 73.8 strokes as his school's No. 3 man, ended the season ranked sixteenth in the nation.

All the walking was taking its toll on his leg, but his stellar play continued that summer in Oregon's top amateur events. He made it to the semifinals of the Portland City Golf Championship at Eastmoreland Golf Course before losing a hard-fought match, one-down. "Casey is a great competitor," his opponent, Greg Hildebrandt, told the *Oregonian*. "I couldn't go to the bank on any hole because he was always grinding."

The highlight of the round was Martin's second career hole-in-one. He was two-down when he sank a seven-iron at the 165-yard twelfth, but it wasn't enough to unnerve Hildebrandt. Martin evened the match by rolling in a twenty-five-foot birdie at seventeen, putting him four under for the last eight holes. But then he made a fatal mistake on the eighteenth when he misclubbed his approach on the 450-yard hole. The ball flew over the green, settling in light rough twenty yards behind it. He chipped short and eventually made double-bogey.

"It was 162 yards with the wind," said Martin, who air-mailed an eight-iron. "I can't believe the ball carried that far, but that's the way it goes sometimes."

A day earlier he had erased a three-down deficit by winning the final five holes for a quarterfinal triumph. The rally included a seventy-foot birdie putt at the fourteenth and a twenty-five-footer for birdie from the fringe at the final hole. "I told my brother on the fourteenth tee that I had only one chance to make three birdies coming in," Martin said. "I made two birdies and, fortunately, that was enough."

Back at Stanford, Martin redshirted and sat out the 1992-93 season, as did teammates Notah Begay and William Yanagisawa. This way they could postpone their fourth year of eligibility to the 1994-95 school year, when a certain young phenom from Southern California would probably enroll. The three golfers had two goals in mind, Martin told *Stanford* magazine, "to get the bulk of schoolwork out of the way so we'd have more time for golf in our last year and—a vague and distant thought—to be there when Tiger Woods came to Stanford."

Between all the golf and traveling, Martin's grades weren't up to his usual high standards. He spent more time hitting balls than hitting the books. "I'm doing okay in school," Martin, an economics major with a 2.8 grade-point average, told the *Oregonian*. "Golf is tough and challenging at Stanford, but so is economics."

It wasn't like he put his clubs away for the whole year. He still practiced a great deal, working hard on a swing change Goodwin taught him. Back home that summer, he won the Oregon Amateur Championship in June, becoming the second Martin in a row to win. Cam had won the same tournament the year before. This time, in a dramatic final, Casey beat David Lebeck on the thirty-seventh hole at beautiful Pumpkin Ridge Golf Club, the site of Tiger Woods's third consecutive

U.S. Amateur victory in 1996. Although the course has hills, they are subtle, and it's not a difficult walking course. Still, Martin's limp became more pronounced as he and Cam, who was caddying for him, came down the final few holes. "He managed okay, but you could see him get tired," Lebeck says. "His pace slowed down. He doesn't walk fast anyway. He can't."

It was a grueling back-and-forth match. Neither led for more than a hole or two. Par won a lot of holes. Indeed, a two-putt par gave Lebeck a one-up lead going into the final hole. "It was a battle of misses," he says. "Sometimes that makes it a better match."

On the par-five eighteenth, Lebeck ripped a 290-yard drive. Knowing he had to make birdie because Martin would, he pulled out his three-wood and tried for the green in two. He flushed it. "I thought it was over," Martin said. "It was so pure." When Lebeck's ball hit the green, however, it kicked left and rolled off the green and down a fifteen-foot embankment. Martin, meanwhile, put his second shot pin-high on the right, just off the green. "I was so exhausted that I just wanted to make contact," he said. Trying to get up and down off a tight lie to a close pin placement, Lebeck hit his chip shot to the other side of the green. Martin then canned an eight-footer for birdie, forcing the play-off.

On the thirty-seventh hole of the match, back at the par-four first, Lebeck just caught the rough with his drive. From there, he caught a flyer with his eight-iron approach. The ball hit the middle of the green, took a nasty hop, and ended up ten yards behind the green. Seeing this, Martin played it safe from the middle of the fairway, hitting a nine-iron twenty feet past the flag. After Martin lagged it down for par, Lebeck missed a ten-footer to tie. Casey Martin was state amateur champ.

"Casey is a great opponent," says Lebeck, now a professional playing the minitours. "He has a great golf swing. It's nice to watch him hit the ball, it is so solid. He hits everything with the upper body. He has to, because he can't work his lower body as well as other people. A lot of the extra movement in the lower body is taken out of the swing, it's all upper-body rotation. And the rotation is so fast. He is an exceptional ball striker. Even when he hits it off line a little bit, it is just so solid the way he hits it. And when he putts good, it's pretty hard to beat the guy."

That match holds very special memories for both players. "I still hear about it because it was such a back-and-forth match," Lebeck says. "It was just a great match and people remember more about it than I do. My neighbor always brings it up." Said Martin, "When Cam and I are retired, we'll both look back and see that we made our mark on Oregon golf."

When Martin rejoined the Stanford squad that fall, his teammates elected him captain. With Begay and Yanagisawa also back for the 1993-94 season, the Cardinal had one of its best teams ever. "They all got along really, really well," Hallock says. "They all were really hard workers. Casey couldn't spend quite as much time practicing [as the others] because his leg would always bother him, but he had such a beautiful swing. He worked a lot on his putting.

"Then Will [Yanagisawa] came in as a transfer. That sort of was like the last click. They just became this incredible team. If someone had a bad round, someone else would always step up. Casey was real consistent. He was never in trouble, very even-keel. Golf sort of reflects people's personality."

Their redshirt plans paid off, too: Woods announced that November he would accept a scholarship offer from Stanford.

Excited about Woods's arrival, they quickly proved worthy of their No. 5 national ranking by winning the prestigious William Tucker Invitational in Albuquerque, New Mexico, in September. For the first time in school history, Stanford shot three consecutive sub-par rounds. They outdid themselves a month later when they won their second tournament of the fall season at home on the Stanford Golf Course, annihilating the twenty-team field and setting another school record. With more than one hundred players competing, four Cardinal players finished in the top ten. Ten days earlier, Martin had won his first collegiate tournament, the Northwestern University Quintessence in Chicago, coming from behind in the final round on the difficult Kemper Lakes Golf Club, site of the 1990 PGA Championship.

Martin's golf game wasn't the only aspect of his life flourishing at Stanford; so was his Christian walk. His faith in Jesus Christ deepened considerably at the school, especially during his sophomore year when he decided to fully commit himself to Christianity. "It was not like God spoke to me from a burning bush or anything," he told *Stanford* magazine. "I just felt I needed to live it as well as believe in it."

Martin became an active leader of the Stanford chapter of Athletes in Action, a Christian Bible study group. When Yanagisawa transferred to Stanford and had trouble adjusting, Martin took him under his wing. He gave Yanagisawa a Bible, took him to church, and brought him to Athletes in Action meetings. Not that Martin didn't know how to party: All he needed was a piano when they were on the road, and you might hear him belt out something like "Great Balls of Fire."

"When you leave home and go to college and you're on your own, there is a lot of temptation going on," says Rudy

Herr, Martin's Eugene youth pastor. "Plus, at a place like Stanford, which is very academic, your belief and faith in God are often challenged by your professors. I went to the University of Oregon, and I know firsthand that you get professors who kind of make fun of you for believing in a God and following Him."

Martin experienced some of that himself. "I understand he took a stand among the members of his team," Herr adds. "Everyone knew right away he was a Christian, and that he didn't do the party thing. He didn't participate in some of the things that athletes and people in general often choose to do when they leave home. Casey chose to walk the straight and narrow according to the way he believes a man of God should live his life, and he has lived it that way. He was a man who lived his convictions. What you see is what you get. It wasn't like he was one kind of guy on the golf course and another kind of guy at church and another kind of guy at school. He was the same person throughout."

As Martin's spiritual faith grew stronger, his leg got weaker. Goodwin testified at the 1998 trial how it deteriorated over the five years that Martin was at Stanford. "I have memories of him struggling to the point where I didn't see how any kid could go on," he said. "But he's a very brave young man. And never, ever, do I remember him wavering or withering or making excuses. But it got significantly worse."

Still, Martin nearly always walked the thirty-six-hole matches. Occasionally, he rode a cart: Pac-10 regulations allow the use of a cart for a permanently disabled player, if approved by a vote of conference coaches. Colleges had to submit a written request and medical statements to the conference office one week in advance. By his junior year in 1994, his cart needs had escalated. Previously, Martin could rest the leg after a match and the pain would ease, although it never went away. But now his suffering was pretty much constant. Even normal walking sent tormenting shots of pain up his shin. The draining of blood from his knee was a weekly occurrence.

He played the last four tournaments of the spring season using a cart. No complaints were voiced by the other coaches—just the opposite, in fact. "Everybody recognized Casey for the person he was, and what he was doing with his life, and every coach, to my knowledge, and every player, wanted Casey in the tournament. They welcomed him there," Goodwin testified. The other coaches never felt that Martin gained an advantage by using a cart. Says Oregon coach Nosler, "The only way a cart gave him an advantage, as far as I'm concerned, was it enabled him to play. Stanford without Casey, we might have had a chance to beat them."

Martin would walk a course as long as he was able, then use the cart to finish whatever holes were left. He wouldn't ride unless he absolutely couldn't go on. It was a point of pride. By midafternoon at the Thunderbird Invitational in Tempe, Arizona, in April 1994, Martin limped through twenty-three holes with the temperature near one hundred degrees. He still had another thirteen holes to go and was really struggling under the weight of his bag. The Arizona State coach felt sick looking at him. "For crying out loud, Wally. Let's get that kid a cart," he said to Goodwin, who just shook his head. He knew Martin would crawl before he'd accept special treatment.

With poor performances by Martin, Begay, and Yanagisawa, the No. 2-ranked Cardinal team withered in the heat and wound up thirty-nine strokes shy of tournament winner Arizona State. It was Stanford's only bad showing of the season, coming on the heels of back-to-back titles at the Pacific Coast Championship and the Southwestern Invitational in March, which in turn had followed a pair of runner-up finishes. Fortunately, the team came home after Arizona to host the next tournament, the U.S. Intercollegiate, where they finished third. Playing as the Cardinal's No. 1 man, Martin led the squad with a three-round total of 213, good enough for fourth place overall.

Then it was back to Arizona in May for the Pac-10 Conference Championship. Stanford held off defending champ Arizona by three strokes on the Wildcats' home course, Tucson National. All five Stanford golfers finished in the top fifteen. The tournament favored deeper teams like Stanford because the top five individual scores count, instead of the usual four at other events. "We're a very deep team," Goodwin told the *Stanford Daily.* "When you have that extra golfer, it helps a lot and hurts some of the teams with less depth. There's really no other visible difference."

Around this time, something strange happened: The NCAA temporarily declared Martin and Begay ineligible. The two All-American golfers, Stanford's No. 1 and No. 2 men, were reinstated several days later, but no explanation was given for their suspension. It turns out upon investigation that Martin and Begay had played golf at a nearby country club with an alumnus, who paid for their lunch and a caddie, which violates NCAA regulations. The players were unaware that they had broken any rules, but when Goodwin found out about it, he voluntarily approached Stanford's department of athletics.

"Thank goodness they had the sense to not suspend them for NCAAs, so they carried it over and suspended them for the first tournament the following year," Hallock says.

A few weeks after the Pac-10 Championships, Stanford returned to Tucson National as the No. 1 seed (and with the nation's second-best scoring average) for the NCAA Western Regional. Nine of the eighteen teams entered would then advance to the NCAA Finals to be contested near Dallas in June. Stanford finished a disappointing fifth, although it was good enough to earn a trip to the NCAA finals. Martin finished at two-under after three rounds, one stroke behind Yanagisawa, who came in eighth to lead all the Stanford players.

"Our entire season has been a story of getting ready to get ready," Goodwin told the *Stanford Daily*. "In college golf, rankings don't mean a whole lot. It's how you do in the NCAAs that matters."

Those 1994 NCAA Championships had the distinction of being the first NCAA Finals ever televised live nationally, courtesy of ESPN. Winning the NCAAs would be Stanford's crown jewel to the greatest golf season in school history: The squad had already competed in fifteen tournaments and finished third or higher in all but three. "We've been practicing as a team since early September," Goodwin said. "The guys have put in a lot of work this year, and I feel that the sport of golf owes them a spectacular finish. Regardless of how we do in the NCAA Finals, this year has been a great year. It's certainly been the best year of my career here."

It would get better. In the second round of the NCAAs, being held at Stonebridge Country Club in McKinney, Texas, Martin's team shot a school-record-low 273. The charge was led by Begay's record-breaking 62 on a hot, windless day. A "switch-hitter" on the greens, he made four birdie putts from the left side and six from the right—ten, in all. (Begay's low round would be a precursor of even better things to come: In

May 1998, he shot a 59 in the first round of a Nike Tour event, joining Al Geiberger and Chip Beck as the only men—at that time—to break 60 in a PGA Tour-sanctioned event.) Martin, meanwhile, shot a 70, a nice recovery from his opening-round 80—his worst competitive day in nearly three years. Goodwin said he was especially proud of Martin. "In my over thirty years as a coach, I would characterize Casey as the toughest athlete I've ever coached," he said.

Although Stanford led the twenty-six other teams heading into the third round, nine teams were within ten shots—striking distance, certainly. Martin proved why he had the Cardinal's lowest scoring average of the season at 72.04, shooting a 68 to lead his teammates. Stanford continued to cling to a small lead, with numerous other schools still bunched closely behind. Five teams began the final day clustered within two shots of the Cardinal's lead. As final-round events unfolded, the only team that came close to challenging Stanford were the Texas Longhorns, backed by a partisan crowd. Despite former U.S. Amateur Justin Leonard matching the NCAA seventy-two-hole record at seventeen under par, the Longhorns came up four shots short. This time it was Yanagisawa who rode in to save the day for the Cardinal, shooting a 64 to lead his team to the school's first NCAA golf title since 1953. Martin, who used a cart all four rounds, had the team's second-best round, an even-par 72 that left him tied for thirty-fifth.

The victory was especially important to Martin, who faced the prospect of losing his leg that summer. He was set to have surgery in July to assess the need for further operations, or indicate to doctors if he'd be better off without the leg. "This has been a tough spring," he told *Golf World*. "I've had torn cartilage, arthritis in my knee, and then shin splints. That was the most painful part. It was so easy to get [those injuries] because the leg doesn't heal easily." He felt that if he returned to school in the fall with a prosthesis, he could learn to play with it. And if he couldn't? "I'm at peace with myself," he said. "If for some reason I can't play anymore, it's okay with me."

Martin's situation really put life in perspective for his teammates. "I think he only tells us a fraction," said Begay. "I think we'll never really know. To have his potential and know in the back of your mind that you might lose your leg is mesmerizing. If I'm out there playing bad and feeling sorry for myself, I'll think, 'What am I doing? Here's a guy that shows so much inner strength.' It makes me feel selfish."

The arthroscopy in July revealed a large, grape-like cluster of abnormal vessels in his knee, Dr. Jones testified at the trial. "[It] was quite dramatic," said the orthopedist, who removed some scar tissue and repaired a tendon.

Despite the operation that sidelined him for most of the summer, Martin had one memorable golfing highlight. Playing in a professional event, the Sunriver Oregon Open, he had two hole-in-ones in successive rounds. In the first round of the tournament, he holed a five-iron on the 188-yard fourteenth of the Sunriver North Course. The next day he sank a nine-iron on the 142-yard third for his fourth career ace. Martin wound up finishing second in the tournament and dismissed reports that he might lose his leg. "I don't know where that stuff is coming from," he told the *Oregonian*. "Sure, there's a chance that some day it might happen, but, if it does, it is way down the road."

A few weeks after his operation, Martin got to see his new teammate Woods in person at the Pacific Northwest Golf Association Men's Amateur at Royal Oaks Country Club in

Vancouver, Washington. "Tell Tiger he'll make a good fifth man for us," Martin said jokingly to the *Oregonian*. When told of Martin's comment, Woods said, "We'll see." Three members of the championship team were returning to join Woods for the 1994-95 school season to give Stanford a stacked deck. "I've met all of those guys, and I already consider them friends," Woods said. "I'm looking forward to fitting right in."

By this time, the Stanford golf team had become a true melting pot. There was a disabled player (Martin); another was Native American (Begay); and a third was Asian (Yanagisawa). Add to that mix the already legendary Tiger Woods, whose mixed heritage included African-American, Asian, and Native American. "We enjoy being different," Martin told *Stanford* magazine. "The average college team is country-club bred. We are unique."

Not surprisingly, they also forged strong bonds that carry over to this day (Yanagisawa is now Martin's roommate, while Begay is Martin's Nike Tour brother, and another teammate, Steve Burdick, is his caddie).

"Casey and Steve meshed together well because they're very religious," Hallock remembers. "They used to read passages from the Bible to Notah on road trips. He'd just laugh."

Martin and Begay also pledged Sigma Chi fraternity together their freshman years and even lived for a year in the frat house, where Martin liked to play the piano from time to time.

"They left because it was too hard to try to concentrate on golf and school," Hallock says.

Martin and the other players even hazed Tiger a little. Like any freshman, Woods had to tote bags on the road and sleep on the rollaway bed. On one trip, a few of the players phoned Woods's room from another. Martin pretended to be

While college golfers often wear shorts in competition when it's really hot, Casey wasn't a big fan of them. This shot of him putting during his days at Stanford hints why. (Photo by Bob Ewell)

a local reporter seeking an interview, and then started asking bizarre questions Woods didn't know how to answer, although he gamely tried his diplomatic best. Martin was unable to sustain the prank and, cracking up, revealed his identity. "It was difficult to haze someone you idolized so much as a golfer," Martin said.

With Tiger on board, the No. 1-ranked Cardinal team won three of its five tournaments that fall. The only time they finished out of the top three was at the Tucker Invitational in Albuquerque, when Begay and Martin were serving their one-tournament suspension for the NCAA infraction back in May.

"It's a completely different world with Tiger," Burdick told *Stanford* magazine. "We're the favorites every time we go out there. It's added pressure, but it's been a good experience."

The team, Goodwin added, "has a chance to make collegiate golfing history. We have three fifth-year seniors [Begay, Yanagisawa, and Martin] and a fourth-year senior [Burdick]— all of them All-Americans. And then we have potentially the greatest golfer who ever lived. This is just a great team."

A highlight of the spring season for Martin was the Duck Invitational at his home course in Eugene—the first time he played there as a Cardinal. While the tournament is held every year, Goodwin was always reluctant to include it on the schedule because of the unpredictable weather in March. "I'm really looking forward to this one," Martin told the *Stanford Daily*. "I grew up there, so it means a lot to me to play in front of my family and friends."

While the team dominated the tournament, Martin didn't play his best despite his vast local knowledge. The pressure of playing in front of a hometown crowd got to him, and he finished tenth. "He didn't look his strongest this week, but he's made a lot of changes in his game and he's still getting used to it all," Goodwin said, referring to Martin's new cross-handed putting style. "Once things come together, his level of play will really start to come up."

It didn't take long. The following month Martin won the U.S. Intercollegiate in his final appearance at Stanford's home course. He shot seven-under 206 to win the individual title by three shots, the same margin of the team victory in the event over Arizona State. And they did it without Woods. With more than seven hundred in attendance—the largest crowd ever to watch a golf tournament at Stanford—Woods strained his right rotator cuff on the first drive of the second round. He played only eleven holes before leaving the course and withdrawing from the event. As a result, the team had to play four-count-four golf, tallying all four players' scores in the team total rather than dropping the worst one as they could have done with a fifth man (Woods).

A similar situation occurred at the NCAA Western Regionals in late May in Albuquerque, where Woods and Martin came down with a combination of food poisoning and dehydration. Martin had to drop out of the competition in the first round. Woods, knowing the team would be disqualified should he also falter, persevered through eighteen holes, often having to lie down or vomit between shots. Incredibly, he managed to make five birdies and shot an even-par 72. After the round, both he and Martin were taken to a nearby hospital. The team, nevertheless, finished sixth and advanced to the NCAA Championships in Columbus, Ohio, the following week.

Despite a less-than-stellar spring season, the Cardinal was the consensus favorite to repeat as champions. All eyes were on

Woods, too, to see if he would capture the NCAA individual crown. But No. 1-ranked Oklahoma State wasn't going to play dead. After two rounds, Stanford was in first place by only two strokes over Oklahoma State, and they increased their lead to nine shots midway through the final round. The Cowboys rallied, however, and Stanford stumbled over the last few holes to send the championship into the first team play-off in the ninety-eight-year history of the tournament. The play-off lasted only one hole: OSU picked up two birdies on the eighteenth hole, while Woods and Begay missed birdie putts of twenty-two and eight feet, respectively. (While Woods led his teammates in scoring with a four-day total of 286, he ended up tying for fifth individually; Martin finished tied for twenty-fourth at 292.)

"We made a remarkable defense, I thought, and with so many guys leaving, it was really emotional," said Goodwin, referring to Martin, Begay, Yanagisawa, and Burdick. "It would have been super to win, but I'm really proud of the guys. They were great this year. And they will continue to be great."

It had been quite a year for the team, witnessing Tigermania firsthand. "That was wild," Martin told the *Oregonian*. "It is unbelievable what he has to deal with everywhere he goes. I saw it firsthand—all the media attention, all the same questions over and over, all the requests for special interviews. Answers began to come out of his mouth like a tape recorder."

Little did Martin know he'd be in the same situation some day.

CHAPTER FIVE

On a Swing and a Prayer

Austin Teague, one of Casey's high school teammates, knew early on that Martin had a pro career ahead of him—not only because he was so mentally tough, but because he was a magician with the golf ball, a Merlin with a Maxfli:

"All of us were fairly decent golfers, but he could hit shots that everybody else would take fifty balls to hit," Teague says. "He could hit a big hook or a big slice or hit it five feet off the ground. He could intentionally top it if he wanted, as a joke. He could pop it straight up in the air to where he could walk a few feet and catch it in his hand. He could do all different types of trick shots like that. I've seen a lot of good golfers, but not too many I know can really make it out there."

Teague knew that he'd be reading about his friend in the papers, much like he did growing up, but in a much larger way. "God has had his hand over Casey," he says. "There is no way he could have gone through what he has gone through if

God wasn't with him. I truly believe that. I am a very strong Christian as well, and I just knew He had a special purpose for Casey."

After graduating from Stanford in 1995 with a B.A. in Economics and as an NCAA Academic All-American, Martin left his amateur days behind. His plan was to give a pro career a try for a few years and see what happened. Still, Martin realized the odds were stacked against him—and not just because of his disability. The chances of any good golfer making it on the PGA Tour are minuscule, let alone for someone who's disabled. "I feel comfortable that, if I can't make it as a tour pro, there are several other things that I can pursue," Martin told the *Oregonian*. "I decided for sure that I wanted to do this after my sophomore year at Stanford. That was one of the reasons that I took a redshirt year before my last two seasons—to try to get my game ready."

There was no question Martin had a special talent for the game. The real question was, Would his leg hold up? Veteran PGA Tour golfer Bob Gilder played with Martin in an event not long before Casey turned pro. "I remember asking his dad what his plans were, because his dad was following him around," Gilder recalls. "I don't think they wanted him to turn pro. Casey's parents were concerned at that point that it would be too much stress, having to walk that much."

Casey was looking forward to turning pro despite his condition, buoyed by how well he had handled the challenge and rigors of collegiate golf, bad leg and all. "I figured the tough part was done; you know, thirty-six holes carrying your bag," he testified at his trial, "and now I could, you know, have a caddie." His first event as a pro came early in that summer of 1995, at the Lilac City Open in Spokane. It was an auspicious beginning. Martin shot thirteen under par and finished fourth. His first pro paycheck was $1,250. "It was a very pleasing start," he said at the time.

In his next event, the Long Beach Open, Martin tied for twenty-eighth and earned $800. He played a few other events that first summer as a pro, and then rested his leg in anticipation of the first stage of PGA Tour qualifying, which for him would be in mid-October at Dayton Valley Country Club in Nevada. If he hoped to make it onto the PGA Tour, Martin would go through three levels of qualifying, and he would need his right leg rested as much as possible for the long haul. The tour-qualifying process is, purposely, a grueling one, designed to weed out thousands of tour aspirants from the few dozen who would be deemed worthy by the Qualifying School for PGA Tour membership. For someone like Martin, fresh out of college, tour qualifying can feel like the equivalent of three years of law school and the bar exam all rolled up into one three-month package. Martin would have to finish high enough in the competitive first stage just to make it to the cutthroat second stage, which in turn isn't as tough as the Q-School's six-round finals. One missed four-foot putt on the 108th hole can mean the difference between a shot at a lucrative PGA Tour career and at least another year on the Nike Tour struggling to make expenses. Factor a crippled leg into all that, and Martin was left with a gargantuan task.

In the first stage of tour qualifying, Martin played exceptionally well, posting a second-round 64 that catapulted him into fourth place at ten under in a field of ninety. He had advanced to the second stage of qualifying with eleven strokes to spare. Too bad he couldn't have taken a few of those with him to La Purisima Golf Course, north of Santa Barbara, site of the second-stage qualifying. Where his second round had made his week at Dayton Valley, it ruined his year at La Purisima: He shot a 77 that led to a five-over-par finish, just two shots away from a ticket to the Q-School finals. Martin's next shot at the big time would have to wait another year, for the fall of 1996 and the next tour qualifier.

By March 1996, the lower part of his leg—his shin and ankle—had started to overshadow the pain in his knee. Walking eighteen holes was more and more difficult, and Martin was becoming more and more frustrated. His doctor, Donald Jones, prescribed a physical therapy program and removable brace to immobilize his leg. Neither helped. That summer, Dr. Jones, a Eugene Country Club member, played a few rounds with Martin to see if he could observe anything about his gait that would help him devise a prosthesis that would make it easier on Martin. First, they tried a shoe insert to keep the tibia from rotating. It didn't provide any relief. Then the orthopedic surgeon placed him in a plastic brace that extended from his toes to the midcalf to stabilize the back of his foot and protect the tibia. Not only did the device irritate Martin's extremely sensitive calf, he found it impossible to make a good swing wearing it. During the two rounds he played with his doctor, Martin was unable to finish all eighteen holes walking. "It was during this time that I became increasingly concerned about the well-being of Casey's lower extremity," Dr. Jones testified at his trial.

Having failed to qualify for entry onto the PGA Tour, or even its Nike Tour "farmclub," Martin in 1996 played—and walked—the NGA/Hooters Tour, a third-level tour (a step beneath the Nike Tour) based in the Southeast. About twenty tournaments comprise a March-to-September season, with an average purse of $100,000. The Hooters Tour has no qualifying school. It's pay and play. Membership costs $1,000 and there's a steep $550 entry fee per tournament. Expenses (room, board, caddies, etc.) typically siphon hundreds more a week out of the bank account. It's a tough place to make a living, but a great place to hone one's competitive game. A golfer has to finish in the top ten out of the 150 contestants to make any kind of "profit." Even those golfers lucky enough to have financial backing live on a shoestring that could break at any time.

"It was grueling," says John Sosa, who's known Martin since the junior ranks and traveled with him on the Hooters Tour. "It was a good experience. We all learned something out there."

Despite his strong Christian beliefs, Martin didn't seem to have a problem playing a tour sponsored by a food chain that ostensibly gets its name from its owl mascot—but really is a thinly veiled reference to the scantily clad, well-endowed young women who staff its restaurants, many of whom worked the tournaments as well. "That didn't bother any of us," says Ralph Howe, another close friend and travel companion. "But we would always get a kick out of putting up the signs for the Hooters Tour Bible Study. We considered just making the sign 'The Hooters Study.' We figured that might get more guys."

Howe, the 1988 Publinks Champion, first met Martin at a Hooters Bible study during Martin's first tournament in Atlanta in March, where Martin had to shoot fourteen under par for the privilege of making $755. Howe didn't learn about Martin's disability until a few weeks later on the driving range at the tour stop in Natchez, Mississippi. As Martin came limping toward him, and with twenty other guys within earshot, Howe screamed out, *"Hey, d'you twist your ankle?"* Martin hobbled over and told him his problem. "I was a little embarrassed, but he handled it great," Howe says. "He just told me he had a birth defect and explained the whole thing, and it clicked right away."

Martin played in thirteen events that year, finishing thirty-third on the money list with close to $20,000 in earnings and a scoring average of 71.5. After his start in Atlanta, he missed the next two cuts but then tied for fifth in Monroe, Louisiana, and picked up $2,464.

The minitours can be a lonely place, Martin quickly discovered. Driving through Alabama, Martin decided to pull over at a truckstop to call Coby McDonald, his old friend. McDonald was surprised to hear from him. They spoke for a minute or two before Martin revealed why he was calling.

"Coby," he said, "I called because I need to apologize for something. Do you remember the party at Jessica Roy's house?"

"Sure," McDonald replied. "That was fun."

Both of them had been in their junior year at South Eugene when their friend Jessica threw one of those typical high school parties at her house one weekend—her parents were out of town. McDonald had brought about a dozen of his favorite CDs to the party. The next morning (about half the guests slept over), he got up and noticed his discs were scratched and scattered all over the place. "I was kind of bummed," he recalls, "but stuff happens at parties. I hadn't thought about it since that night."

There was genuine remorse in Martin's voice as he stood in the phone booth at the Alabama truck stop and explained what happened.

"Joel [Rubenstein] and I took them outside with some other guys and we were playing Frisbee with them," he said. "We were the ones who ruined them and we didn't want to tell you."

McDonald couldn't believe what he was hearing. "Casey, first of all, that was a long time ago. I appreciate you apologizing, but I don't care," he said. After that they both kind of laughed for a minute or two, and then McDonald said, "Casey, what in the world made you pull over to a truck stop in Alabama?" Responded Martin: "When you drive around playing the Hooters Tour, you spend a lot of time in the car. You can only listen to so much radio and you start thinking about everything."

His conscience clean, Martin missed only one cut in his next eight events and almost won in July in Charlotte, North Carolina, where he shot 66 in the first round and ended up tied for the lead at fifteen under at the end of regulation. But he lost on the first play-off hole to Dicky Thompson, who rolled in a thirty-footer for birdie. Martin's second-place check was worth $8,755. Ironically, the hilly course had been one of the tougher ones they had to walk all year.

"You can interpret that as a tribute to him and his ability, or you can flip it around and say, 'Wait a second here. If he can walk that one, he can walk anything.' You know what I'm saying?" says Tim Singer, the tour's director. "But I think it was more of a tribute to his athleticism and character. The course is brutal. There was one hole where you tee off down into a valley and you have to hit way up this hill to the green. Some of those guys were struggling to get up that hill. Even the guys with caddies struggled to get up that hill."

Bad leg and all, Martin was on a roll. The next week in Fayetteville, North Carolina, he tied for third when he shot in the 60s all four rounds, finishing at seventeen under and winning $4,500. He had just picked up a new Great Big Bertha driver and was hitting it a ton. The persimmon-wood-playing Sosa couldn't believe it.

"Man, you wouldn't believe this thing is so easy to hit," Martin said to him one day. "Look at this." He then proceeded to lace a couple of three-hundred-yard-plus drives. "Look at this, off the deck," added Martin, who then hit it just like he did off the tee. Thought Sosa, who played at the University of Texas, "Man, if I could hit it like that, I'd shoot nothing! This is a serious weapon right here." He wasn't just referring to the club. "I mean, not only does he have the talent, but this club is a match," he says. "He was just killing it."

Sosa, along with Howe and another friend, Bill Hoefle, played a lot of practice rounds with Casey. The bets were usually limited to short-game challenges after each hole, where you could lose or win five to fifteen dollars over the whole round. "We would hit all kinds of pitch-and-run shots, bunker shots, lob shots," Sosa says. "It was a good way to push each other and stay sharp. We didn't want to dig into each other's pockets. It was just something on the line to test our nerves."

After his second- and third-place finishes in 1996, Martin played in only two more Hooters events, missing the cuts in both. He rested his leg at home in Eugene, getting ready for the first stage of the PGA Tour Q-School in October, again at Dayton Valley Golf Course. But with a second-round 80 and three others over par, he wound up tied for thirty-ninth at thirteen over, ten shots too high and twenty-three shots higher than in '95.

Facing another year on the Hooters Tour, Martin placed a call to tour director Singer on October 29, asking him if he could use a cart the following season. "We spoke about it at length," Singer says. "He told me about his situation and said that he believed the only way that he could continue his career would be with the aid of a golf cart. I told him that the request caught me off guard, and I was not able to give him an immediate decision on that. I didn't even know if I was the person to make such a decision. It was a very professional conversation, a very rational conversation. It was a very cordial conversation. We were both afraid to hurt one another's feelings, but it was simple business. At the time, I considered Casey and I pretty good friends, and I still do. He may not [feel the same way], but I certainly respect him as a person even more than as a golfer, and that is not an insult to his golfing abilities."

Before hanging up, Casey told Singer that he had legal representation and that they would probably be contacting him. Singer discussed the request with his staff, the tour's owner, and just about everyone else, including the PGA Tour. "It was a situation that had not presented itself to the PGA before, but they felt that it was just a matter of time," he says. A short time later, a letter arrived at his office near Atlanta from Martin's attorney, William Wiswall, citing the Americans with Disabilities Act. Also enclosed was a letter from his doctor describing his medical condition. He turned everything over to the tour's counsel, who denied the request based on some non-golf-related ADA decisions.

Singer was convinced that Martin would gain an advantage if given a cart, although he could see the flip side of it, too. "Needless to say, it was a very uncomfortable situation to be in, especially because of the friendship I thought I had with Casey," he says. "We both attended the Bible study group together, so our relationship went a little beyond that on the golf course. But he took it so well, it was not something I lost sleep over every time I saw him. It was like, 'That was the decision, so let's go tee it up.' "

Singer believes the decision was the right one. "There is no doubt in my mind that if some guy goes out and walks eighteen, and the other guy goes out and rides eighteen, the guy riding is more refreshed or at least doesn't get as tired as the guy walking. One thing to point out about our tour is, unlike a PGA Tour playing up in Michigan, Canada, and Minnesota, or what have you with all these northern properties, we're in Dallas and Houston and Myrtle Beach in August [all locales noted for their heat]. It's definitely a factor."

Naturally, Martin was disappointed. "He considered filing a lawsuit against the Hooters Tour in order to have a precedent," Howe says, "but it wasn't the right time." That time wasn't far off.

"He had asked me, 'Do you think there is going to be a big problem with this if I try and push it and ask for a cart?' " recalls Hoefle. "I said, 'Hey, look, Case, everybody who knows you out here knows that if it was perfect, you would want to walk, you would want to do it the way everybody else does. The pain you go through and the handicap you have—I have no problem with you wanting to have a cart.' "

Martin, no doubt, envisioned the day when he'd have to take on a much bigger golf entity than the Hooters Tour. While staying with a host family during the Hooters stop in Sikeston, Missouri, Martin and Hoefle were watching a U.S. Open telecast in June 1997 when the subject of their conversation turned to playing the PGA Tour together in 1998.

"Well, I can't do it unless I have a cart," Martin told him.

"What do you mean?" Hoefle asked.

Said Martin, "Well, I have already talked to some lawyers and, if it comes down to it, I am going to try and get a cart to play. If I'm going to play every week and try to make my card, I've got to have that."

Hoefle wasn't surprised by what he was hearing. "I don't know how I would feel if I didn't know Casey as personally as I do, but it was not even an issue to me," says Hoefle, who was a bit taken aback with PGA Tour member and diabetic Scott Verplank's outspoken opposition to Martin (he testified on the PGA Tour's behalf during the trial). "I know him pretty well, and I respect Scott as a golfer. He's a great guy, but I think he is way off base if he thinks that the trials he goes through as a diabetic and the physical problems he had measure up to what Casey has been through. I don't think that is even comparable.

"You need to spend one week with him, living with him, to understand what his handicap does to him physically. First of all, the guy cannot sit still for more than two hours at a time. The leg does not allow him to be comfortable. Even twenty minutes is difficult. He has to be moving, changing position. Normally, after we are done playing and in the hotel from seven until we go to bed, we used to just veg out on the bed and watch TV. Now he can't do it. He has to get up and move around. I knew that things were bad when one night I woke up to the sound of this shriek. He had gotten out of bed and was going to the rest room and nicked his shin on the table. He was floored. For you and me, it might be just a ding and it hurts for a second, but he was totally collapsed on the floor in pain."

Though he popped Advil like candy—three or four at a time—it didn't do much good. "By now he is probably pretty much immune to it," Hoefle says. "I remember looking in his travel case one time and seeing this huge bottle. He went through quite a bit."

Martin's pain was becoming so chronic that he was in agony even at rest. Concerned, Melinda Martin spoke to his doctor about putting her son on narcotics. She had heard about a physician who prescribed a low-methadone treatment program for a patient with a similar problem. Dr. Jones had Casey evaluated to see what might be done to manage his pain. The result of the extensive consultation, which included psychological testing, determined that since Casey was such an over-achiever, the use of time-contingent narcotics, or methadone, around the clock wouldn't work. "[It] may relieve his pain to the point where his aggressive nature would result in self-harm," Dr. Jones testified at his trial.

The consultation also revealed that Martin had a sleep disorder that led to exhaustion syndrome the following day. "Evidently, for patients who have chronic pain for long periods of time, some of the neurotransmitters in the brain are depleted," said Dr. Jones. "This results in the need to waken multiple times during the night. Because they wake multiple times during the night, they are exhausted the next day, like anyone who doesn't sleep." Casey passed on the opportunity to take sleeping pills because the potential side effects, such as struggling to get up, would interfere with his golf game.

Walking eighteen holes, meanwhile, was really starting to affect his performance on the course. Martin played in just fourteen Hooters events in 1997, making the cut in seven of them, with three top tens (he also played some events on Florida's Tommy Armour Tour—they allow carts). Playing in only one of the last eight Hooters events, Martin finished sixty-third on the money list with a little more than $11,000. Fortunately, the tour allowed carts during practice rounds and the Wednesday pro-am, so that saved some wear and tear on his leg. But his condition varied from day to day, tournament to tournament.

"There were definitely times after the rounds I would say, 'Hey Case, how are you feeling?' " Hoefle says. "And he would say, 'My leg is really bad today,' or something of that nature, and you just don't understand why it is different some days. Maybe he stepped on it wrong or accidentally hit his club against his leg, or whatever it was."

Most of the players carried their own bags during the tournament, but Martin always tried to use a caddie. If he could find one, that is. "He could not possibly play without a caddie," Howe says. "It's not like the Nike Tour or the PGA Tour. We relied on high school or junior high kids to come out and caddie. Before school got out in June, it was pretty tough. It's not like caddies were standing around and you only had to ask them. You had to go to a member or the pro and ask. There were quite a few times when Wednesday night came and he still didn't have a caddie, and he would mention that at the Bible study and we would pray about it. The next morning you'd look down the fairway and see Casey with a caddie. It was really neat."

Sosa got a kick out of some of the caddies Martin would recruit. "He would always get these little boys around thirteen to fifteen years old, even younger, twelve years old," he says with a chuckle. "He would come back and say, 'Hey, boys, you would never guess who I have for a caddie. This poor little guy, the golf bag is bigger than he is. He's working so hard.' He would have to pull his strap up as tight and as high as he could so the kid could carry that bag. And his driver was about as tall as he was, too. He felt so sorry for them. I mean, he did all he could for them, made sure they had something to eat and drink. Paid them pretty well, too."

There were a few times, though, Martin didn't find a caddie, and that was rough. "I would almost cry watching him, want to help him, and not be able to do anything," Howe says. "I remember playing a practice round with him one time when we couldn't get a cart. He had his bag on his shoulder that day, and up and down the hills, his knee would lock up on him. It is incredibly painful for him, and he just buckled over and almost went down to his other knee. He would grimace and drop his bag and stop for a minute. Pick up the bag and keep going and not say anything. But you could tell by the look on his face, he was in a lot of pain. He was frustrated."

Most of the guys drove between stops, but Martin usually flew because his leg couldn't take the six- to eight-hour car trips. At the different events, Martin would split fifty-dollar– or, God willing, forty-dollar–a-night rooms with one of the others. Upon check-in, the first thing he did was request more pillows, since he used five of them to elevate and cushion his leg at night. Despite his trouble with sleeping at night, they all loved having him as a roommate. Although Martin spent much of the time grimacing on the bed with his leg elevated (sometimes he'd lie backward on the bed with his right leg up the wall), he never complained. "He is just a great guy," says Howe. "He's very intelligent, very funny, and he is basically lighthearted. He is fun to be with."

He also didn't hog the bathroom. Because he took off his stockings to shower, his leg would quickly fill up with blood. "So he would take a real quick shower, but even then it would be very painful," Howe says. "He would come out and hold the leg up in the air and let the blood flow back down, and then he would put the brace back on."

Howe has since retired from the life of a touring pro, partly due to the fact that he's a newlywed, for which he has Martin to thank. The two were at the tour stop in Memphis and were going to pass through Nashville where Howe's wife-to-be lived. "I knew I wanted to marry this girl, but I was kind of chicken to ask her out," Howe says. "I was traveling with Casey and he kept bugging me to ask this girl out and get together. He finally left a note on my bed that said, 'Call Melinda, Chicken Boy.' My nickname became 'Chicken Boy.' "

Martin shamed him into calling. If only it were that easy for his friends to get him to ask a girl out. His standards are so high, friends say, he really struggles finding Ms. or Mrs. Right. "He is so picky about girls," Sosa says. "He wants a girl that is a Christian, a virgin, everything like that. He goes, 'Man, just look at [women] today. Do you think I can find somebody? And then if I did, would she be everything I had ever wanted? Would she want me the same way? I may never get married.' "

Martin is apparently looking for a fifties-type girl in a nineties world. "He wants to find somebody who is a Christian, saving herself like he was saving himself for that person," Sosa says. "That's a really serious deal and a very important thing to him. Today, it's like 90 percent of girls have probably slept with somebody. That's his conviction and devotion to Christ. That's the same way it was for me before I got married."

It's not like Casey didn't have opportunities to meet the right girl. Oftentimes, the golfers were hosted by Christian families in different cities. In return, they'd buy food and cook dinner a couple of times, such as chicken in Thai peanut sauce or chicken enchiladas. Though Martin is a man of many talents, cooking isn't one of them. "He actually was a recipient of great food," Sosa says. "He got involved in it, but he pretty much assisted. 'Tell me what to do, I'll help out.' "

Martin contributed in other ways. Staying with a family in El Paso, Illinois, during the 1996 season, Hoefle and Sosa cooked up one of their big meals while a huge storm raged outside. Afterward, Casey gave an impromptu performance on an upstairs piano to the accompaniment of the thunder. "Everybody congregated up there and we started singing some songs," Sosa says. "He was showing off a little bit, even though he didn't mean to. It was a blast. I was amazed. He is so good. It was one of the best nights we had. Good food, good fellowship, the family was awesome. It was great. Casey was the life of the party. We were the cooks, he was the show."

He didn't do too badly that week on the course, either, shooting two over par and tying for thirty-third, good for $830. But life on the road was harder for Martin than it was for the others.

"He would get tired quickly," Sosa says. "The rest of us would be like, 'Hey, let's go do this,' and he would say, 'No, that's okay, guys, I'm going to go back. I feel tired, I'm going to rest my leg a little bit. I've been on my feet too long.' He couldn't do everything."

Like go to the movies and stay for the whole picture. "If it's not any good, he'll walk out," Sosa says incredulously. "And I mean, I've never really done that before unless it's a really bad movie. But it could be a decent movie at least and he would still walk out. You have to understand, Casey is pretty much uncomfortable most of the time. We always had to sit on the right, on the aisle. Actually, if the movie theater wasn't full, Bill and I would sit toward the center and Casey would sit in the same row but fifteen chairs on the right all by himself, propping his leg up on the chair in front of him. We would look at each other occasionally, nod our heads and flip up our hands as if to say, 'How ya doing?' "

If one of his friends had posed that question for real, they didn't always get a truthful answer. Although Martin is generous to a fault, he isn't always philanthropic with his feelings. There was one time, though, when Martin poured out his feelings to Sosa when they were staying with Sosa's relatives during the tour stop in Louisville in June 1997. One night, they had to share a king-sized bed, and neither one of them could sleep. "We just laid there for like an hour and a half, thinking the other was asleep," Sosa says. "It was about one-thirty in the morning, and I said, 'Hey, dude, you awake?' He goes, 'Yeah, man, I can't get to sleep.' I'm like, 'You're kidding! Neither can I.' After that we ended up talking for another hour and a half, about our golf game and our plans for the future."

Martin did some real soul-searching that night. He had missed the cut in seven of his last ten events and was starting to doubt his ability. "We were both kind of frustrated at that time," Sosa adds. "He was a little concerned. He's asking me, 'John, you're married, and you have two children, and when you're not playing [well], you're not making a dime. How can you justify staying out here when you have a family back home counting on you, and you're not playing any good?' It was a hard question for me."

It was one that Martin was asking himself, no doubt. "He basically felt like, you know, if he didn't make it within the next year, he was pretty much done," Sosa says. "He was like, 'It just gets so monotonous. It's too much of a job when you're out there and you're missing cuts. It's lonely.' He didn't know if this was the kind of life he wanted. He was thinking if he didn't make it soon, he wanted to settle down—meet a girl, get serious, and get married. He really looked forward to having a family and finding the right girl for him. He goes, 'Well, look at you. You've got a family, you've got kids, you've got everything you want except you're not on the [PGA] tour. I don't have anything.' "

As they lay there in the dark staring at the ceiling and into their futures, Sosa told him he had too much talent and had overcome too much to give up. Says Sosa, "I told him he shouldn't worry about it, that he should just try his hardest and keep pressing on. 'You'll come to a point where you really know in your heart whether you should stop or not.' We were trying to figure out what God wants us to do. That was one of his deals, 'If God wants me to play, I'm going to make it. If He doesn't want me to, then obviously it's not going to happen.' "

God must have been listening to that late-night conversation. Casey's life was about to change forever.

CHAPTER SIX

Reluctant Rebel

Martin was prepared to walk away from the life of a pro if he didn't make it on tour with his third try at Q-School. He filled out his application, ponied up his $3,000 entry fee, and signed his name on the form with the clause, "Use of golf carts is prohibited during the final qualifying stage."

That October, he teed it up at the first stage of qualifying at the Dayton Valley Country Club in Nevada. He opened with a 68 and ended up shooting 283, good enough to tie for thirteenth and advance to the second stage. Two or three shots higher and the world probably would never have ever heard of Casey Martin, since only twenty-three of the ninety-one players moved on. This was going to be his last shot at the big time.

At the second stage in mid-November at Bayonet Black Horse golf course in Seaside, California, with his dad caddying for him, Martin shot a 74 in the opening round, followed by a pair of 73s. With one round left, he wallowed in forty-fifth place; only twenty-three players would advance. The next day would decide the rest of his life. He needed to turn it up a notch in the final round if he were to realize his dream. That night, his dad told him how proud he was of him and that, no matter what happened, the family support would always be there. Casey turned in a gutsy 69, one of only four players out of seventy-eight to shoot in the 60s that day. While his Stanford teammate Notah Begay won the tournament at seven under, Martin tied for twelfth at one over. He made the cut by three shots, one of twenty-three players to move on to the finals in December.

Bob Gilder, who also finished at 289, was one of the first to congratulate Martin. "Oh yeah, he was excited," he says. "First or last, you're still in. Any time you advance in something like that, you're relieved and happy."

Ironically, the first stages of Q-Schools are the only PGA Tour events players can ride in a cart. (Carts are also allowed during Monday qualifying, but those fall under the domain of the PGA of America—a separate organization from the PGA Tour.) Officials feel that requiring the eleven hundred original contestants to have a caddie places too much of an economical and logistical burden on them. And prior to 1997, the 168 contestants could even ride in the finals, but the tour changed the rule to better mirror conditions that players face on tour. The decision was made long before Martin qualified. "A lot of players voiced to me in 1995 that they felt that not requiring caddies, having carts, did not create the same challenge level in the finals of the qualifying tournament as we have on the PGA Tour," Commissioner Tim Finchem testified during the trial.

After making the finals, Martin asked the tour for a cart. He was turned down. With the finals just a week or so away, he made another call, this one to William Wiswall, his Eugene attorney, and a longtime family friend and Eugene Country Club member. On November 24, Wiswall wrote to Edward Moorhouse, the PGA Tour's executive vice president and chief legal officer, requesting a cart for the final six rounds, which were set to begin December 3 at Central Florida's Grenelefe Golf and Tennis Resort. (Also included was a letter from Martin's doctor describing his medical condition and indicating he could not walk the requisite number of rounds.) The first hint of potential legal problems for the tour was contained in the last paragraph. "Your consideration is greatly appreciated as Casey would like the matter, at this point, to be decided in his favor discreetly, as opposed to taking action under the ADA," Wiswall wrote, referring to the Americans with Disabilities Act.

Just as the Civil Rights Act of 1964 protected the rights of minorities, the ADA, which Congress enacted in 1990, was designed to protect the rights of the disabled. It centers on improving the life of the disabled in public-access areas. For the most part, though, ADA is applied in much more mundane ways than in Martin's case. It's the reason buildings have wheelchair ramps and wide toilet stalls. Businesses and other public entities must make reasonable accommodation for the disabled unless they can show that such a modification would fundamentally alter their business activity. Included in the ADA are provisions relative to employment laws as they affect the disabled.

After discussing the situation with Finchem, Moorhouse replied the very next day. His message: Take a walk, literally. Not only did he remind Wiswall that Martin had contractually agreed, as verified by his signature on the entry form, to walk in the last phase of the tour's qualifying tournament, but he also contended that professional sports competitions were outside the scope of the ADA. The next day, the Wednesday before Thanksgiving, Wiswall walked the block from his office to the U.S. District Court and filed a motion, asking for a preliminary injunction that would allow Martin to use a cart. The Friday afternoon hearing two days later caught the PGA Tour off guard. They scrambled for two Portland lawyers to represent them in U.S. Magistrate Tom Coffin's wood-paneled courtroom housed on the first floor of the courthouse. In the hour-long session, they first tried to argue that Oregon had no jurisdiction over the PGA Tour, which is headquartered in Florida. But the judge ruled that Martin lived in Eugene; that was enough. They then tried to show that the ADA didn't apply since they were a private membership organization, citing a federal appeals court ruling that the NFL was not covered by ADA.

"The PGA's position is that these participants are all athletes," said Michael Francis, representing the PGA Tour. "It is fairly grueling. By the end of a round, golfers begin to tire. If Mr. Martin were to use a golf cart, that would provide Mr. Martin with an unfair advantage. It fundamentally alters the nature of the game." To counter, Eugene lawyer Jacquelyn Romm cited other cases that contradicted the tour's position, and she noted that the ADA specifically forbids rules that "tend to screen out" individuals with disabilities. A good swing and low score, not the ability to walk, are the traits of a good golfer, she argued. Allowing Martin to use a cart would not cause undue hardship on the PGA, Coffin determined, and he ruled swiftly in favor of Martin. "Clearly, the balance of hardship tips overwhelmingly in favor of the plaintiff (Martin)," he said.

The opening salvos in one of the most compelling, publicly divisive sports-related cases had been fired. In a sport where the biggest conflicts are usually over pin placements and the length of the rough, this was a doozy. Professional golfers are, by nature, not a controversial group. They like the status quo. The members of the PGA Tour are so homogenous, all you have to do is flip the bill of your cap up *à la* Jesper Parnevik, and you're a real rebel. But their predictability is a big part of their credibility. The papers these days are filled with boorish conduct of professional athletes, but you'll probably never read about a tour player getting arrested or cross-dressing.

With his country-club background, Christian beliefs, and classic swing, Martin fit right into that group. A more appealing plaintiff you could not find. That's why it was so difficult for him to finally move forward with his case. He and Wiswall had discussed the ADA before, but Martin declined. By the summer of 1997, however, he began to soften his position. Martin had come to the proverbial fork in the road over lunch with Wiswall at a Thai restaurant in Eugene.

"Bill, if I don't make it on tour, I'm giving up golf," he said. "It's just too hard."

There wasn't much to be said after the tour had turned down Martin's initial request for a cart. The time had come to take the issue before the courts. It wasn't a decision Martin and his family made lightly. "It's kind of tough," King Martin told *People* magazine. "We've never been sued or sued anyone in our lifetime, and never dreamt that we would. But we're not sure that we're outside the law, so that's why we're doing it. It was a last resort."

When word of the injunction came down, Casey and his dad were headed to a different battlefield—the Q-School finals, a grueling 108-hole, six-day marathon, and the biggest tournament of his young life. The final stage of Q-School is the most pressure-packed tournament the pros ever play. He would have to perform under the microscope, too. The story was irresistible to the sporting press, who descended in numbers on the Grenelefe Resort in Haines City, Florida.

"I don't think anyone realized the amount of attention he was going to get," says his Hooters Tour buddy, Ralph Howe. "He might have been a little bit nervous by all the attention, but he was not unnerved. He was ready. As a professional golfer, you live for situations where people come to watch you."

Martin wanted to be recognized for his ability, not his immobility. Still, he was very relieved to have the temporary use of the cart and, at the same time, apprehensive over the upcoming lawsuit. "There was not an ounce of malice or anger in the lawsuit," Howe adds. "The lawsuit was something he did not want to do. He did not want the attention. It was just that if he doesn't have a cart, he cannot play competitive golf—and he could lose his leg."

Gilder, who had dinner with the Martins one night that week, knew something about taking on the tour. He was a plaintiff in the Ping lawsuit against the tour in the late eighties when they tried to ban the club manufacturer's square-grooved irons.

"That was probably the worst part of my whole career," Gilder says. "People picking sides against you. 'How can you do this? You're going to ruin the tour, you're going to ruin golf.' I had to listen to the same thing with Casey: 'What is the tour going to turn into? Everybody is going to drive a cart! That doesn't look good for the sport.' "

To his credit, Martin didn't let the suit's gravitas get him down. "I'm sure it was hard for him," Gilder says. "But I'll tell you one thing: I have never seen a kid with a better attitude. He is so up. I'm sure he has had his down times, but I've never seen a man with that much of a positive attitude. An attitude of, 'Whatever happens, happens, and no matter what, I'm going to go on. I'll just leave it up to them. If they're not going to let me, fine. If they let me, fine.' Either way, no decision was going to get in his way."

Finchem instructed Bill Calfee, the tour's executive vice president for competition, to comply with the court order and allow Martin to use a cart. On Tuesday, however, right before the first round was to begin on Wednesday, Scott Verplank brought up his own condition as a diabetic. He asked Finchem if he could use a cart since Martin was getting one. To be fair, Finchem allowed anyone who wanted to use a cart the right to do so. But only a small minority of the 166 players did, perhaps fifteen to twenty (an exact number was unavailable, since the tour said it didn't keep any records). What is for sure is that Verplank, in a cart, went on to win the tournament by six shots over runner-up Blaine McCallister and another three strokes over two players tied for third.

Gilder was one of the many who walked. "I think there is more to the game by walking," he says. "I see the game better. I see what I'm doing. It gives me time to think. There is something about riding a cart, in my opinion, that takes away from the reality of the game. Part of the game is walking and seeing everything. When you walk, you get a sense for the golf course. You lose some of that perspective when you ride. I'm sure Casey knows the difference, because he has walked most of his life."

Moments after winning the Nike Tour's Lakeland Classic in Florida in
January 1998, Martin was already preoccupied with his next big
challenge—his upcoming trial against the PGA Tour. (AP/Wide World
photo by David Mills)

110

Although it's questionable what difference having a cart made in the scores of the other players who took one, there's no question that Martin benefited from the use. There's no way he could have walked six straight days and finished as well as he did. Gilder played a practice round with Martin, who had to quit after nine holes even with a cart. The swing is never what causes the pain. In fact, swinging the club is one of the few moves that doesn't bother his leg. You never see him wince in the backswing, for instance.

"When I'm swinging well, the leg seems fine," Martin told *Stanford* magazine. "And yet it is there in my subconscious, and when I'm not playing well, the thought is always there that it could be the leg."

Alternating between the par-72, 7,301-yard West Course one round and the par-71, 6,717-yard South Course the next, Martin was one under through four rounds. He finished with a pair of 70s and missed his PGA Tour card by only two shots. Still, he earned a full exemption onto the Nike Tour and was now just a step away from "the Show." His play was almost incidental, however, to the larger issue of his getting a cart. "Apparently, this is bigger than I thought," he told the *Register-Guard*, after his return to Eugene. "It doesn't seem to be that big an issue to me. I just need a cart to ride. I guess it's going to be bigger than that. I would love to walk and blend in with everyone else. I have no desire to stand out that way. But I have no other options."

Martin spent the rest of December at home in Eugene trying to prepare for the first Nike event in Lakeland, Florida, the second week of the New Year. Also on his front-burner agenda was his preparation for the upcoming trial, scheduled to begin February 2. He wasn't able to play many, if any, rounds at

Eugene Country Club, since the club wasn't allowing cart use due to the wet winter. So, weather permitting, he spent most of the time on the practice tee and putting green. "Watching him practice and walk off and on the range was painful," ECC member Bruce Chase says. "He limps a lot more than he used to."

Like the rest of his family, he spent a lot of time giving interviews (his mom, Melinda, did fourteen in one day). Wiswall felt it was necessary to get Casey's story out to prevent a "hostile work environment," since the PGA Tour "was attempting by its media releases to discourage touring professionals from testifying for the Plaintiff, was attempting to discourage other lawsuits by golfers and to generally garner public support for its stated position that 'everyone must play by the rules,' " he wrote in court filings. "Even being provided cart accommodation would not give [Martin] an equal opportunity to compete if he was ostracized by his fellow touring professionals, harassed by the PGA Tour tournament officials, or annoyed by members of the gallery. The implication of the PGA Tour in its public statements and implied in Court was to the effect that [Martin] was dishonest in the making of his claim because it would allow him to avoid having to play by the rules and it was important, therefore, to make the public and professional touring golfers aware that [Martin] had a major disability of significance and one that could ultimately lead to amputation if not provided with a cart."

The interior of Wiswall's office became quite familiar to Martin. One day in January, Casey sat across the desk from his attorney who spoke the words he did not want to hear. "What we have to do," Wiswall said, "is show them." He was hoping that a video of his leg would be dramatic enough that the tour would be forced to settle the lawsuit out of court.

Martin worried about his privacy, that the video might end up on the evening news. But there was no other way, especially if they hoped to avoid the expense and publicity of a trial. Standing before a video camera, Martin removed his slacks and two elastic stockings. Seconds later, his knee began to balloon to twice its normal size, and a number of veins appeared on his shin. The back of his thigh turned bluish-black. "Talk about your leg," Wiswall prompted him. Said Martin, matter-of-factly: "It will keep going until I sit down."

As the trial date loomed, the issue continued to grow. In grillrooms all over the country, talk invariably turned to Martin. Most amateurs were in favor of letting him ride, since that's how so many of them play the game. The professional ranks were split down the middle.

"Golf is an athletic sport," Ken Venturi said in *Golf World*. Venturi should know: He overcame heat exhaustion during a thirty-six-hole final round to win the 1964 U.S. Open at Congressional Country Club. "I feel sorry for anybody who has a handicap, but I'd have to say, 'No,' for two reasons: Where do you draw the line, and how do you cope with it in the major championships—with the galleries at the Masters or the terrain at the British Open?" Curtis Strange, editorializing in his *Golf* magazine column, wrote: "Those of us who are getting a little older, who grew up having been taught about golf's history and values, have the responsibility of preserving the game's integrity. That means walking.... In a sport full of bad backs, bad hips, and bad knees, I believe we will open a can of worms by making an exception."

Others were in Casey's corner. The Martin supporters included Tom Lehman, a player-director on the PGA Tour policy board whose brother, Jim, runs the player agency that includes Martin as one of its clients. "If it's the only thing keeping him from being out on the tour, then let him ride," he told *Golf World*. "If the talent's there—if the desire's there—I would hate to prevent him from the chance. Shoot, let him play." And wrote John Cook in *Golf World*: "To deny a young man with this kind of talent goes against everything the PGA Tour stands for. After years of marketing itself with the catchy phrase, 'Anything's Possible,' Casey Martin has proved that anything really is possible.... The guy isn't riding in a cart to take advantage of a competitive situation, but to eliminate a competitive disadvantage. Believe me, there is a big difference."

Wiswall tried to settle the case out of court by sending Martin's medical records and the videotape to William Maledon, the tour's chief outside counsel. He wanted Maledon to show it to Jack Nicklaus and Arnold Palmer, who were going to testify on the tour's behalf. Maledon returned the material unopened. From the tour's point of view, Martin's condition was irrelevant. They accepted the fact he had a disability, and they wanted the issue to track on a more abstract plane.

King Martin lobbied Nike head Phil Knight to intervene. John Jaqua, a lifelong friend of King's and an original Nike board member, was the go-between for King and Knight. King brought two videos with him to the January 5 meeting with Knight at Nike headquarters in Portland: one showing his son's poised appearance on the Golf Channel, which nicely encapsulated the issue; the other showing the powerful images of Casey's leg after he took off his stockings in the tape Wiswall made. Martin told the *Register-Guard* that Knight was visibly moved.

"I told him I was there with three requests," King said. "That if he sided with us, my dream would be that he would be an advocate for us with the commissioner" in trying to

Casey Martin boosters popped up everywhere in early 1998, even at Bermuda Dunes for the 1998 Bob Hope Desert Classic—even though Martin wasn't entered. (Allsport USA photo by Jon Ferrey)

reach a settlement. Secondly, King hoped Knight would make a public statement on Casey's behalf. Lastly, King asked about the possibility of an endorsement affiliation with Nike. Knight agreed immediately to the first two requests, and forwarded the sponsorship proposal to the appropriate Nike executives for consideration.

By the end of the week, with Casey in Florida playing in the Nike Tour's first event of the season, Knight still had not spoken with Finchem. Casey's agent, Chris Murray, telephoned King from Minneapolis to report a sponsorship offer from a computer software company. "We were facing heavy legal expenses, and it was one we were inclined to take. But I told Chris that I didn't feel comfortable doing anything without letting Nike know," said King. The next day he had his Nike contract offer (a reported $50,000 to $75,000, with incentives), and the following week Knight hooked up with Finchem, expressing his support for Martin and seeking to avert a trial—to no avail.

The tour and Wiswall did work out an interim agreement to let Martin use a cart in the first two Nike Tour events. Limping to the first tee at the Grassland's Golf and Country Club in Lakeland, Florida, in the opening round of the tour's opening event, Martin was well aware that, because of the controversy, he was about to take the most scrutinized swing of his life. *Don't top it, don't shank it,* he thought to himself. *Don't shoot 90 with all these people watching.*

He needn't have worried about that. After his opening drive, Martin hopped in his cart and went on to birdie three of the first four holes. One particularly interested spectator that day was Charlie Owens, who first raised the issue of using a cart in competition more than ten years ago. Owens, who has a fused left knee and other leg problems stemming from a 1953 parachuting accident in the army, won two tournaments on the Senior Tour in 1986 using a fifty-two-inch putter and a cart. That was the year the Senior PGA Tour tried to ban carts except for players with certified medical reasons, because, as Arnold Palmer said, "It's just not very attractive to the galleries or to anyone seeing professionals riding down the fairway." But the ban reportedly never took effect because of fears that marquee names like Sam Snead would bail if they couldn't ride. The USGA has never allowed carts, however, in the Senior Open, and in 1987, the organization turned down Owens's petition to use one. To protest, Owens walked the first nine holes on crutches before he withdrew.

"I took a mountain of Motrin when I was playing golf," Owens said in *Golf World*. He lives in Tampa, just thirty miles from Lakeland, and introduced himself to Martin after he teed off on the eleventh hole. "I couldn't afford to get into a legal battle.... People say it's an advantage to ride. Well, if you're disabled, it's not an advantage. For a person with a handicap, getting in and out of that golf cart is like wrestling a bear."

Martin wound up shooting a six-under 66, which left him one shot off the lead, but heavy rains washed out half of the first-round's play, causing contestants to play catch-up the rest of the week. Martin didn't complete his second-round 69 until Saturday, when he played twenty-five holes, including fifteen holes of his third-round 65. As he rode, the rest of the field slogged through wet conditions over the 7,040-yard course. Gary Koch, the forty-five-year-old NBC golf analyst, had to play thirty-two holes Saturday. He said a cart might have helped him. "Yes, I think it would have been an advantage to use a golf cart," he said. "Was it an advantage for him? I can't

In more ways than one, Martin was all alone in front as he went on to win the Nike Tour's 1998 Lakeland Classic in Lakeland, Florida. (Allsport USA photo by Andy Lyons)

say. When I finished [on Saturday], I went straight home and sat in my Jacuzzi for half an hour. Every bone in my body ached. Of course, I'm forty-five and out of shape and not used to walking eighteen holes, let alone thirty-two."

But it was Martin's length and power (he averaged almost 283 yards driving)—not his cart—that helped him overpower the soggy conditions. Because he had to keep his cart on the path, he estimated that he walked at least one hundred yards on every hole. By Saturday night, he found himself drained and exhausted.

"It was double pressure for him, triple pressure," his caddie, Boyd Cornwell, told *Golf World.* "At night he wasn't sleeping, and he had all these things going through his mind. He goes back to his hotel and the phone rings all the time. [On Saturday] he said to me, 'Boyd, please pray for me. I didn't sleep last night, and I'm having an awful time.' He just kept hitting those good shots. The cart had nothing to do with it."

Someone else who was struggling was Steve Lamontagne, who was three shots behind Martin at thirteen under at the start of the fourth round. A painful ingrown toenail on the big toe of his right foot necessitated Novocain shots all week. By Saturday night, it had become so bad he had to have surgery performed right on the course inside the medical tent. "The doctor numbed me up and pulled it out," he says. "It wasn't too thrilling." The next day, Lamontagne had to cut away the top of his shoe to play the final eighteen holes. (His situation was later brought up at the trial.)

In the final round, Lamontagne kept the pressure on Martin, his playing partner, making four birdies in a six-hole stretch on the back nine. When Martin bogeyed the par-four fifteenth hole and Lamontagne birdied, Martin's lead was cut to one. Then he showed the resolve that has helped him overcome so much in his life. On the very next hole, another par-four, Martin "hit one of the best iron" shots all week, sticking a wedge from 135 yards to within four feet of the pin and sinking the birdie putt to move to nineteen under. The turning point came on the seventeenth, a 410-yard par-four. After hitting his approach, Martin was left with a tough, downhill twenty-footer. He rolled it ten feet past the hole. When Lamontagne made birdie, Martin was looking at a two-stroke swing. But he made the comeback putt to retain a one-shot lead going into the final hole. Matching pars on the unreachable par-five eighteenth gave Martin his first tournament victory since college.

"That putt on seventeen really won him the tournament," says Lamontagne, who admits he doesn't think a cart would have helped his final-round 67, nor does he begrudge Martin using one. "I can't say I feel poorly about it. I don't know if he had an advantage, because of the problems with his leg. I don't have any bad feelings towards that. I did what I had to do to play golf and play well. I was pleased with how I played. I wish it had turned out different, but that's the way it goes."

"A weight has been lifted," Martin said after his victory. "All the stuff about the court and about me playing in a cart, it kind of weighs on you emotionally. Just to win, it's an amazing relief. I'd really written off doing anything substantial. It's a new experience. I was overwhelmed I was able to do as well as I did."

His victory, worth $40,500, bolstered his contention that the only thing keeping him from a career as a successful professional was a cart. "There was a lot of self-doubt about whether I was good enough to play with these guys," he said. "I love playing golf, and if I don't have a cart, my leg gets so painful, it's not worth it. I hope it all works out. I'd love to make a career out of this."

Finchem wasted little time in releasing a statement after his win. "The fact remains that Mr. Martin participated and won while using a golf cart under the terms of a court order," he said. "The outcome of this week's Nike Lakeland Classic doesn't in any way affect the PGA Tour position relative to the use of carts."

At the beginning of the week, all anyone could talk about was Martin's use of the cart. By the end, his use of his clubs got equal attention, at the very least. Through it all, Martin never lost his sense of humor. During the first round, he was driving down a cart path when he passed a two-man TV crew lugging heavy camera equipment around.

"You guys need a cart to carry all that stuff around," Martin said to them.

"We asked," one of them replied, "but the tour won't let us have one."

"Let me introduce you to my attorney," Martin said. "He'll fix you right up."

CHAPTER SEVEN

David vs. Goliath

Bill Wiswall didn't take the case just because he was a close family friend. Nor did he take the case for all the publicity he would get out of it. He took the case in part because he suffers from a condition somewhat similar to Martin's. He has malformed veins in his brain, although he's able to control it with medication. A tall, burly man, he is also a fairly decent golfer (now a twelve-handicapper; he once was a one) whom a teenaged Casey even caddied for once or twice when his leg was stronger. Wiswall's son, Mike, played on the golf team at South Eugene with Cam Martin. A longtime Eugene resident, he graduated from the University of Oregon in 1956, before getting his law degree there in 1962.

In the early seventies, Wiswall made national news when he obtained an acquittal in a drunk-driving case on the grounds of insanity. But his highest-profile case prior to *Casey Martin v. PGA Tour, Inc.* came in 1986 when he devised a novel theory to win a large monetary settlement for a shooting victim's widow and child. After a deranged sniper shot and killed an Olympic athlete from Jamaica while he was training in Autzen Stadium on the Oregon campus, Wiswall showed that the man was insane and, therefore, had no intention of killing the athlete. Since it was an accident, he was able to collect for his client under the homeowner's policy of the killer's wealthy father.

Wiswall is a former criminal defense attorney who now specializes in personal injury and divorce law. Although a seasoned litigator, he's not a disabilities expert. That explains why he brought into the case Martha Walters, who heads a Eugene law firm skilled in civil rights and employment law. In November 1997, she had won a $1.4 million award on behalf of a fired Oregon State softball coach.

Leading off for the tour was William Maledon, a litigation specialist from Phoenix who once clerked for U.S. Supreme Court Justice William Brennan. He represented the tour against Karsten Manufacturing in the late eighties. That's when the tour tried to ban the company's square-grooved irons because they produced so much extra "bite" in apparent violation of USGA design specs. The clubs were particularly helpful out of the rough, thereby negating the advantage of driving the ball in the fairway. Karsten won an injunction barring enforcement of the ban and settled out of court. The tour ended up withdrawing the ban.

But that dry, technical case didn't have the emotional public relations wallop that *Casey Martin v. PGA Tour, Inc.* did. "I've lived in Eugene for twenty years and I've never seen anything like it," says Kristi Anderson, the court reporter during the trial. "This was the biggest thing to hit Eugene, and it'll probably be the biggest thing to hit Oregon for quite some time now. How often does Oregon make the national news? Everyone was talking about it. It came up in every single conversation you had with anybody. It was one of the most interesting trials I've ever worked on. It raised so many issues."

Indeed, the case sparked heated debates not just about the very essence of golf, but about the rights of the disabled, and government and judicial interference in pro sports. If anybody was capable of sorting out the issues, it was Judge Coffin, say those who know him. Tall and thin, Coffin is a highly respected Harvard Law School graduate. "He's brilliant, very succinct, and to the point," Anderson says. "He's also fair." Supporters of the tour's position were bothered by the fact that the judge wasn't a golfer, but as the boys' varsity soccer coach at a local high school, he knew more than a little about athletics. He took the team to a state championship in 1996. As a federal prosecutor with twenty-one years' experience before becoming a judge, Judge Coffin knew something about the law, too.

Although Martin's case was the first lawsuit in the nation in which a professional athlete invoked federal disability laws in order to compete, it wasn't the first involving a golfer seeking to use a cart in a tournament. In 1991, Dr. Dan C. Bird of California asked the USGA if he could use a cart to enter a U.S. Senior Open qualifier. When the USGA denied his request, he filed a complaint with the U.S. Department of Justice, which decided against taking any action after receiving a thirty-nine-page letter from the USGA. The letter became the tour's blueprint for its defense. There was one big difference: Bird was an amateur, while Martin was a professional whose livelihood depended on playing golf. Martin knew that if he were going to have any real chance to make it as a pro, he needed a cart.

Without the use of one, the most he could play would be about one tournament a month. And there's no way he'd make it against the best players in the world as a part-timer. "I'm going to have to get out there week after week and battle it out," he said in the *Register-Guard*.

Like any good lawyer, Maledon tried to get the case thrown out by claiming that the tour was a private club or entity exempt from the ADA. More reasonably, he wanted the judge to agree that the area inside the ropes—the actual playing area for the competing golfers—is not a place of public accommodation. He lost on both counts. "[The tour is] part of the entertainment industry, just as all professional sports are," Judge Coffin said, after hearing arguments in the case at a January 26 hearing. "Without public participation, there would be no PGA Tour, Incorporated. The tour is essentially a commercial enterprise."

The rulings paved the way for the nonjury trial and tilted the playing field heavily toward Martin. He already had a home-court advantage, and now he had a huge lead even before the teeing off. The *coup de grâce* was applying the ADA to the areas of play, badly undercutting the tour's case. Maledon argued the holes are no more public than the kitchens of restaurants or the players' dugouts at baseball stadiums, but Coffin disagreed. He based his decision on the list of public accommodations that appears in the ADA, which includes restaurants, movie theaters, bowling alleys, private schools, and golf courses. These businesses can't have "zones of ADA application," he said in his written findings.

Coffin continued: "What the PGA also overlooks is that people other than its own tour members are indeed allowed within the boundary lines of play during its tournaments.

What if a member-golfer opted to hire a disabled caddie? Once the caddie steps within the boundaries of the playing area of the golf course—a statutorily defined place of public accommodation—does he step outside the boundaries of the ADA simply because the public at large cannot join him there? If this were the law, how could such be reconciled with the inclusion of private schools, whose corridors, classrooms, and rest rooms are clearly not accessible to the public, on the list of places of public accommodations?"

"We're glad, with this much invested in it, to at least get the chance to decide in a full-blown trial whether the law is on our side or not," King Martin told the *Register-Guard*. "The first round is ours."

It was the second time in as many days the Martins had good news to celebrate. The day before Casey's deal with Nike was announced, chairman Phil Knight noted his company's strong relationship with the PGA Tour in a prepared statement, then said, "We think they are wrong in this particular case. . . . We believe Casey should be allowed to chase his dreams. He provides an inspiration for us all."

The company unveiled a thirty-second TV ad featuring a close-up of Martin saying, "I don't want them to take pity on me because I limp around. You might as well chase your dreams while you're young before it's too late. I'm not going to let my leg stop me." Referring to all the new Swoosh goodies—such as shirts, shoes, and outer gear—he was getting, Martin, as he headed into the hearing, said, "It's like Christmas every day."

Before the actual start of the trial, both sides went heavy on a PR offensive. Martin's victory in Lakeland dramatically raised his profile and that of the case, as well. All of a sudden, he

By mid-January 1998, Martin was answering questions about his ADA-based lawsuit against the PGA Tour. Such is the case here at a press conference during the week of the Nike Tour's South Florida Classic in Pompano Beach. (AP/Wide World photo by Gary I. Rothstein)

wasn't just another victim whining about not getting a fair chance; he was a clean-cut, articulate, and sympathetic character with a real talent for the game. He may have missed the cut in the second Nike event, but he made the grade as far as the national media were concerned.

Martin was getting more airtime than Monica Lewinsky and Vernon Jordan put together. And it wasn't just the sporting press. Everyone from CNN and NBC to *Time* and *People* magazines wanted interviews. Even Geraldo and *Hard Copy* wanted a piece of him. "It feels like the whole country is watching. I wasn't ready for this," said Martin, who received favorable press for the most part, although he was thrown a bit off track when he appeared on CNN's *Crossfire,* a Washington-based political talk show that goes out of its way to be argumentative. Conservative co-host John Sununu, former First Golfer George Bush's chief of staff, acted like he was cross-examining Martin on the witness stand. "Jose Maria Olazabal developed arthritis [in his foot] and had to drop off the tour," Sununu said in his gravelly voice. "Should he have been permitted under your criteria to use a cart?"

"That's a tough question for me to answer," responded Martin, appearing via satellite from Deerfield Beach, Florida, the night before the start of the Nike South Florida Classic. "First of all, he doesn't have a disability. He just has a problem."

Sununu countered: "But he could have been born with an arthritis gene that showed up late in life. The fact is, somebody is going to have to make these tough decisions. It ought to be within the PGA structure itself, wouldn't you agree, rather than the courts?"

Martin looked very uncomfortable under the grilling. "Again, I'm a person with a disability, and I believe under the

129

Americans with Disabilities Act, industries or corporations such as the PGA Tour need to accommodate people with disabilities."

"But, Casey," said Sununu, cutting him off, "The ADA doesn't talk about disabilities you're born with versus disabilities you acquire; it talks about people with disabilities. So if a disability is the issue, Jose Maria Olazabal's qualifies just as much as yours under the act."

"Then great, let him play," Martin said. "That's fine."

Not everyone in Washington was unkind to Martin. The author of the ADA, Iowa senator Tom Harkin, and former Kansas senator Bob Dole, who is himself disabled, came to his defense. Dole wondered aloud if the letters PGA stood for Please Go Away. In late January, after the tour lawyers deposed Martin until ten o'clock one night, he grabbed a few hours' sleep and then drove one hundred miles in the rain to Portland to catch a 7:00 A.M. flight to Washington for a press conference with the two politicians. "He's absolutely exhausted," King Martin told *Sports Illustrated*, "but he wouldn't have a case if there wasn't an ADA. So he felt compelled to go."

Martin's situation was exactly what Harkin had in mind, he told the Associated Press, when he wrote the act, which was designed to open all aspects of life—sports included—to the disabled. It's not fair for groups such as the PGA Tour to opt out, he said, adding, "I think the PGA stance could send the wrong message to millions of Americans with disabilities." Edward Eckenhoff, president and CEO of Washington's National Rehabilitation Hospital, told *Golf World*, "To shut Martin out because of something he never asked for—his disability—doesn't sound like America to me. We're not asking that [Martin] be given strokes or the opportunity to play from the red tees. Just give him a lift and see what he can do."

While in Washington, Martin also received some support from the world's all-time leading money winner in golf, Greg Norman, who had encountered his own problems with the tour when he tried to start a world tour several years earlier. Norman's world tour, to be backed by the Fox Network, never made it off the ground after the PGA Tour intervened to say its membership players wouldn't be released to play the number of events Norman was talking about. In 1997, however, the PGA Tour announced its own world tour of sorts, which would involve the designation of a few selected events, starting in 1999, as world-championship events—which together would

Martin is flanked by former senator Bob Dole on the left and Iowa senator Tom Harkin on the right during a January 28, 1998, news conference on Capitol Hill. Harkin, author of the ADA bill that became law in 1990, and Dole emerged as two of Martin's many supporters. (AP/Wide World photo by Dennis Cook)

be the seeds, perhaps, for a full-fledged world tour someday. Norman wasn't even consulted before that announcement was made. So if the Shark was looking for payback, his siding with Martin could be construed as such. Norman called Martin on the phone to give him encouragement. "He said he wanted me out there, and that really made me feel good," Martin told the *Oregonian*. "He also said the tour had asked him to give a deposition on its behalf, and that he had told [tour officials] he wouldn't be a good one for them to use."

The tour reportedly had a staffer tape Martin's media interviews while he was in Florida and then send them back to tour headquarters in Ponte Vedra Beach, Florida. Finchem and his legal team could peruse them, perhaps looking for any Martin statement that could then be used against him in court. The tour also released a three-page statement explaining its position on the use of carts in competition and circulated articles supporting its side, such as one from *Investor's Business Daily* that said, "It's easy to sympathize with Martin. But his case shouldn't be resolved in a courtroom. It's based on a rotten law. . . . [The] ADA is surprisingly vague and overly broad, leaving regulators and the court with near-total discretion to decide how the law should be enforced." And the *Fort Lauderdale Sun-Sentinel* editorialized: "Carts in professional and top amateur golf competition are as out of place as bicycles in the Boston Marathon, and a federal judge shouldn't be afraid to say so."

Finchem even wrote his own article for the Associated Press. "While we believe our action is in the best interest of the PGA Tour, its members, and the entire sport of golf, it nevertheless is a very difficult path for us," he said. "We know that a successful defense of our sport's competitive integrity would likely affect the professional playing career of a fine young man. In our attempts to maintain fairness and an even playing field in our competitions, we realize that what is good for the group is not always good for every individual in that group."

For every article supporting the tour, there were ten others castigating it as shortsighted, anachronistic, and just plain dumb. "An exception for Casey Martin will not hurt the sport," the *New York Times* said in an editorial. "It will make the PGA look wise and compassionate. It will add diversity and interest to a game that doesn't need to be any more dull or homogenous." The tour became an easy potshot, as suggested in the *Orlando Sentinel*: "Rolling out all the heavy artillery, such as anti-cart legend Arnold Palmer and a team of high-priced lawyers, to thwart young Martin, couldn't be more unpopular with the masses than if [Tim] Finchem ordered all the songbirds at tournaments shot as nuisances."

The week before the case went to trial, the PGA Tour was in Pebble Beach for the AT&T Pebble Beach National Pro-Am, where the players had plenty of time to sit around and discuss the case during rain delays. "We were all talking about it," actor Jack Lemmon says. "All the players I spoke to, like Peter [Jacobsen] and Payne Stewart, felt two things. First, there was no way that they (the PGA Tour) were going to win, and they were thrilled for Casey. But, number two, they were worried about what it would do to the game of golf."

If the lawsuit were a golf match, Martin would have played the front nine flawlessly and the PGA Tour would be two down at the turn. But most matches are won and lost on the back nine, and the trial was yet to come.

CHAPTER EIGHT

Casey's Case

The PGA Tour's legal team and the national media set up command posts at the Eugene Hilton, just down the street from the U.S. District Courthouse. To accommodate all the press, the February 1998 trial was moved to a larger second-floor courtroom. Forty print, TV, and radio journalists—representing, among others, CNN, ESPN, the *New York Times*, and *USA Today*—filled more than half the seating, leaving only about twenty seats for the general public. Two sketch artists, one for the Golf Channel and the other for ESPN, were also present. Court TV petitioned to get the trial televised, but Judge Coffin turned them down, much to Martin's relief; he didn't want the videotape of his leg aired.

The video was exhibit A the first day of the trial. The ten-minute tape left little doubt about the seriousness of Martin's illness. The courtroom watched in darkened, stunned silence. Martin kept his head down for the most part, quietly weeping at his lawyer's table. His mother, Melinda, seated a few feet behind him, also sobbed. The evidence was presented during the testimony of Dr. Donald Jones, Martin's highly regarded orthopedic surgeon, who looks after a number of University of Oregon athletic teams. He helped establish that Martin was, indeed, legally disabled. Standing outside the witness chair and using an anatomical chart, he explained Martin's vascular malformation to the court. "But probably more significant is what this drawing doesn't show, and it doesn't show degenerative changes in the knee as a result of his condition," Dr. Jones testified, noting that the bleeding inside the lining of his knee had caused considerable atrophy. "And likewise, it doesn't show that this bone, the tibia—the major weight-bearing portion of the lower leg—is now beginning to resorb [or dissolve] and lose bone stock."

When Wiswall attempted to play the video, Maledon objected because Martin made some comments on the tape that Maledon claimed would be hearsay.

"Have you reviewed it?" the judge wanted to know.

"No," Maledon said.

Incredulous, the judge responded, "You haven't seen this?" Coffin overruled his objection since Maledon would have ample opportunity to cross-examine Martin about his comments.

As he perused Martin's records, Dr. Jones then discussed his patient's twenty-three years of medical treatments, starting from the time his office first saw Martin at the age of three on July 21, 1975. "No less than twenty-one physicians have had direct or indirect input into his care," Jones said. "His parents became increasingly apprehensive about Casey's condition, not only because of bleeding around the [birthmark], but because

136

he also experienced severe right-knee pain, which limited his activities even at an early age."

Not until Martin was five, and only after vascular studies, was a specific diagnosis made. With no surgical options available, the only treatment was compressive stockings. Dr. Jones went on to describe the three arthroscopic operations Martin had: in 1982 at age ten, in 1988 at age fourteen, and in 1994 at age twenty-two. "Over the next two years the knee pain became increasingly more incapacitating," Dr. Jones added. "However, the knee discomfort was soon to be overshadowed by his severe tibial discomfort."

To illustrate his point, he presented a series of X rays, the first one taken when Martin was nine in 1981: It showed fairly good bone stability. By December 1989, when Casey was seventeen, the X ray showed bone erosion, which increased significantly over the next sixteen years.

"Now, this raises a number of concerns for me as an orthopedist," Dr. Jones said. "Number one, if Casey should fracture this, which is a real possibility with just daily activities, being able to go in and fix this bone, because of the poor bone stock, would be very difficult. But it raises other concerns, as well . . . that blood is infiltrating into the muscle, destroying the muscle and the nerve, and rendering the leg functionless." Blood clots were also a concern. "We all know that if you get blood clots, quote unquote, in your brain, the results can be migration to the lung, significant illness, and even death."

"Can some of the danger be removed if he's allowed to ride a cart as opposed to walking?" Wiswall asked.

"I think this is a progressive problem, and I'd certainly like to see Casey with his leg elevated as much as possible. The engorgement of the bone with blood is one of the problems created, which creates resorption of the bone," answered Dr. Jones, who was worried enough about the complications of Martin fracturing his leg that he devised a small tag for his golf bag that explains his problem "so that if he should break his leg at a golf site, they would have some idea of the underlying problems."

In all likelihood, Martin would have to have the leg amputated, perhaps even above the knee. Various experts around the country recommended "rodding" the tibia, but they were very quick to point out that it carries the risk of amputation, so Martin has not pursued that option.

When Wiswall tried to ascertain from Dr. Jones whether Martin was at a "competitive disadvantage" on the Nike Tour if he didn't have use of a cart, Maledon objected, but Coffin overruled him. "I feel that because of Casey's pain and because of the potential for the extremity to fracture, he is at a disadvantage as compared to someone who has a normal extremity," Dr. Jones said.

Maledon seized on this statement in his cross-examination, especially as it concerns fatigue and the various fitness levels of Nike Tour participants. But Dr. Jones deflected his attempts to draw him into a debate, claiming he wasn't an expert on fatigue. Likewise, Maledon wasn't able to elicit from Dr. Jones that he recommended Martin give up golf. "I have informed him of the potential risk and complications, including fracture, and then I let Mr. Martin make a decision as to whether or not he should choose to play golf or do anything else," he said, before considering whether playing golf is a serious risk to Martin's safety. "I think walking across the street is a serious risk to Mr. Martin's safety at this point. I think Mr. Martin's leg at this point in time is at risk for fracture with virtually any activity."

Not long into the trial, it was clear that the scales of justice were tipping in Martin's favor. Here he is seen outside the Eugene, Oregon, courtroom walking alongside his attorney, William Wiswall, a friend of the Martin family and an avid golfer as well. (Chris Pietsch/ the *Register-Guard*)

As dramatic as Dr. Jones's testimony was, it was Martin's brother, Cam, who provided the day's most emotional moments. "I just remember, early on, I guess, when I was about five and a little older, I could—I remember him particularly at night, up crying a lot, several times, maybe more, a week," he said. "And [he] did that for a long period of time." Calling Casey "too tough for his own good" when it came to golf tournaments in high school, he also recalled how much more difficulty Casey was having with his leg at that period than when they were younger. "His condition," Cam continued, "as I've seen it on a daily basis as we were growing up, has gotten just progressively worse. Younger, there seemed to be time frames where he would have periods of—better periods with less pain—that were longer. And those periods of no pain began to shorten, and basically all the way, you know, until early college where I wasn't living with him anymore. And I can still tell after that. He was in more pain more often. . . . Whether it was going to a restaurant and having to sit [with his legs] under a table that was too small. . . . And particularly after rounds of golf he was in pain. And most often I could tell at night."

But Casey's pain paled in comparison from then until now. "He's absolutely in the most pain I've ever seen him in this last year, in 1997," Cam said, noting how difficult even everyday things are for his brother. "He's always watching out for it. . . . In riding [in a] plane, he's always got to be—if you are viewing the cockpit, he's got to be on the left side of the plane with the aisle seat or he cannot—he can't sit there. It's extremely difficult for him to drive in a car. Every time I've ever driven anywhere with him, I'm the one driving because he's got to stretch his leg out and elevate it. It's constant. Every day there's something that he has to function differently than I do with two healthy legs. Every day." Cam did a good job of keeping his composure until the very end of his direct testimony when Wiswall showed him a 1976 picture of his then four-year-old brother confined to a wheelchair at the San Diego Zoo. With an emotionally stricken face, he acknowledged that the picture was indeed of Casey.

A little earlier, Cam had asserted that most professional golfers—including himself, when he played the minitours—would much rather walk than use a cart, something Martha Walters stressed in her opening statement on Martin's behalf. "Your Honor, the evidence will be that walking is an advantage," she said, turning the tour's argument on its head. "In the

Senior Tour, where golfers can choose whether to use a cart or not, many choose to walk. Hale Irwin, the leading money-maker on the Senior Tour in 1997, who earned more money than Tiger Woods did on the regular tour, chooses to walk. Your Honor, we believe that the evidence will be that it is not the competitive advantage that Mr. Martin would hypothetically have that concerns the defendant, it is the image that the carts project."

She also addressed her client's debilitating condition "that requires him to dig deep down; not just to rely on tenacity, guts, determination, but to draw upon real courage when he steps up to the tee in each tournament and into this court asking that he be permitted to pursue a career as a professional golfer on the PGA Tour. . . . Your Honor, the evidence will be that the defendant has publicly proclaimed in its ad campaign anything is possible. Here, allowing Mr. Martin the use of a cart and thereby a career is not only possible, it's reasonable, it's required, and it is right."

In the opening statement for the tour, Maledon didn't take issue with Martin's disability and his contention that he couldn't walk four rounds of golf, because that wasn't the central issue for the tour. The crux of the case, he said, was whether waiving the walking requirement for him would fundamentally alter the nature of competition on the PGA Tour and its Nike Tour. Since the PGA Tour's modern inception in 1968 and the Nike Tour's in 1990, players have walked, he said, as they have in virtually all elite tournaments through the ages, long before TV came into play. "This is a rule of substance, not of style. [The purpose] is to add to the competition a relative additional degree of adversity through the fatigue and stress and other factors that are brought about by walking the twenty to twenty-five miles that is required of the competitor over a four-day tournament. . . . It builds up so that in the fourth day, the effects of it are most extreme. . . ."

"This case is not about Casey Martin," he added at the end. "This case is really about whether a substantive rule of sports competition should be altered to meet the needs—unfortunate needs, but nevertheless, the needs—of a particular individual or individuals. No court has ever done that, and we submit, Your Honor, that the evidence in this case will not support doing so here."

Nike Tour member Eric Johnson, who grew up in Eugene and is a friend of Casey's, was the first pro to offer testimony on the issue of walking on the second day of the trial. "I consider walking as part of the game only as the (means) to get to the next shot," said Johnson. He walked in the 1997 Q-School finals, like the vast majority of players, even though they had an opportunity to use a cart. "I prefer to walk, probably for a number of reasons. One, it's how I've played golf most of my life, and it keeps me in a rhythm. . . . Weather's a real large contributing factor in walking. I would much rather walk if it was raining, because I'm able to stay under my umbrella and not get as wet, my equipment stays dry, those types of things."

After asking Johnson about everything from his pre-shot routine to spikeless shoes, Wiswall wanted to know if he ever felt "stressed out" after walking eighteen holes. "Not physically," said Johnson. Wiswall also asked him if he were "graded" in any way on the manner in which he walked, and Johnson responded to laughter, "No. Thank goodness. I walk funny."

In his cross-examination, Maledon first established that Johnson was not an employee of the Nike Tour. If he were, it would have added significance as far as the ADA is concerned. Further along, Johnson confirmed that he did not get to pick and choose which rules he could adhere to. He also agreed that all athletes bring different physical attributes to the start of a competition, such as the fact that John Daly drives thirty yards farther than he does on average.

"And when you showed up for the tournaments in which you and John Daly were both playing last year on the PGA Tour, you were not given a thirty-yard advance from where you would tee off compared to Mr. Daly, were you?" asked Maledon.

Judge Coffin overruled Wiswall's objection that the question was argumentative, and Johnson answered. "Of course not," he said.

"You and Mr. Daly had to play by the same rules, correct?" Maledon continued.

"Correct," Johnson replied.

The next witness, golf historian Robert Murphy, testified by speaker phone about how some aspects of the game, like the stymie and the U.S. Open's thirty-six-hole final, have changed over the years. Also testifying by phone was Martin's college coach, Wally Goodwin, who talked about the deterioration of Martin's leg while at school, resulting in his use of a cart the last couple of years. Under cross-examination, Maledon got a surprising answer when he asked the coach whether he'd object if the University of Arizona team members all got to use carts and Stanford had to walk. "Not at all," said Goodwin, speaking from Tucson. "I'd like to see if we could beat them in their carts. That would be exhilarating competition for me."

Also testifying on Martin's behalf was Gary Klug, a University of Oregon professor with a Ph.D. in physiology.

He characterized golf as a sport with a "low level of intensity" that isn't "an activity that would be considered to be particularly taxing from a physiological perspective." A golfer walking eighteen holes would typically burn about five hundred calories, or "less than a Big Mac," so he doubted there was a cumulative effect from walking eighteen holes four days in a row. But he couldn't determine the comparative levels of fatigue between one golfer who rides and another who walks, because fatigue is a matter of perception. It's affected as much by a person's motivation and desire as it is by his or her physical conditioning.

Maledon couldn't even get him to agree that a person who walks four to five miles experiences some measure of fatigue. "No fatigue at all?" asked Maledon, a bit surprised. Klug responded: "I couldn't agree with it unless I knew something about the other factors involved. For example, how long did it take, how large is the individual, how heavy—excuse me, what kind of fitness level the individual has."

The best witness, however, for Casey Martin was Casey Martin, who took the stand on the third and final day of testimony on his behalf. But first, Wiswall questioned two people by phone with relevant lawsuits: Harry Toscano, who had filed an antitrust lawsuit against the PGA Tour; and Valentin Rodriguez, a lawyer who successfully represented a disabled teaching pro against the PGA of America under the ADA in 1995. Toscano, a former PGA Tour player who now plays occasionally on the Senior Tour, wants to change the eligibility requirements of the Senior Tour and allow an increase in more qualified players. What was most interesting about his comments was the revelation that three players on the Senior Tour have used devices to accommodate medical infirmities in direct violation of rule 14 of the USGA Rules of Golf, which says a player may not wear any artificial device or unusual equipment during a round. Lee Trevino and Jerry McGee have worn a rigid plastic brace on their thumbs.

"Many players on the Senior Tour have asked about it, questioned it, and complained about it. But the rules officials have permitted it," said Toscano, who also noted that Dave Stockton builds up the shoe on his left foot because his left leg is shorter than his right. That is also a violation about which players have complained.

Rodriguez's client, Gary Lawton, was an aspiring club pro who wore a prosthesis; his left leg was amputated above the knee. Part of the testing process is the ability to play thirty-six holes in one day with a score of 156 or less. Like the PGA Tour, the PGA of America also has a "no cart, must walk" rule. Over the strong (but overruled) objection of Maledon, who called it "hired testimony," Rodriguez told how he appealed to the PGA for a modification of the rule. "I basically cited the Americans with Disabilities Act as the grounds for the accommodation," he said, noting that no legal action was taken. "Their board took it up and approved it, apparently with the help of their legal counsel, who advised them of our position under the [ADA]."

Not the kind of person to draw attention to himself, Martin had hoped against hope that the PGA Tour would have done the same thing. Yet here he was, limping to the stand to be sworn in at the trial he did not want, with the eyes of a nation—and much of the rest of the world, even—on him. Over the next hour and fifteen minutes, he shifted several times in the witness chair trying to get comfortable physically. There was no getting comfortable emotionally, however. After Martin gave a general background on himself, Wiswall presented some photographs of him as a junior golfer holding a trophy and his leg in a wrap. He also presented the court with an advertisement for EZ-GO golf carts picturing the Big Three: Jack Nicklaus, Arnold Palmer, and Gary Player. And then Martin began to describe his medical condition.

"There's a lot of pain involved," he said. "Oftentimes severe. A lot of discomfort with the stocking I have to wear. That wears on you, both mentally and physically. There's also a stigma attached when you limp and no one else does, and you're kind of known as a person with a disability, that I have to deal with."

He also spoke about his trouble getting a good night's sleep because his leg starts to throb, the pain coming from deep within the bone. "When I go to bed, my leg, the blood pools in my leg and it hurts. And I wake up oftentimes because of that. And also the condition I've been having in my shin and tibia, with the bone deteriorating due to the hemorrhaging, I wake up oftentimes with severe—severe pain in my shin. And it's hard to sleep." Even though Martin sleeps with pillows between his legs, he has awakened many times just because his legs were touching. "My leg's extremely sensitive. Any touch to it just sends me off.

"My condition has been steadily worsening for about the last four years, I'd say. Ever since—well, it's always been bad, but I can remember midway through college I started really suffering, especially in my shin, in a way that I hadn't experienced before." It was especially so when he walked hilly golf courses. "It stresses my leg considerably. When I walk on uneven terrain, my shin just—it screams out, basically, is how

146

I like to explain it. It lets me know that—that I'm doing something I shouldn't be doing."

Wiswall then guided Martin through his recounting of some of his medical procedures, such as his three arthroscopic surgeries and his use of two full Jobst stockings for the last nine years. "I used to wear [only] one," he said. "It's just not enough anymore. I have to wear two stockings extremely tight, because without it my leg will swell up to such an extent, it just feels like it's going to blow up." The only time he takes them off is to shower, because his leg balloons up so quickly without them. He has to lie two or three times under the running water—something his brother, Cam, didn't find out till that day seated in the courtroom. "Normally, I don't like to take long showers because of it," Casey said.

It was a clear indication how difficult even the littlest, overlooked things in life can be for him. Slipping behind a steering wheel was another everyday occurrence he couldn't take lightly. "I don't like to drive because of the swelling that goes on," he said. "When I drive the car, I drive with my left foot many times, just to put my right foot up so the swelling is reduced. . . . It's extremely painful when I have to keep my leg bent [at a ninety-degree angle]. I have to do a lot to accommodate that when I drive, any—I just can't sit still, as I'm sure you've all unfortunately witnessed right there. I can't sit still because my leg swells and it feels horrible. And that's constant. I'm never free from that."

Wiswall then sought to negate the tour's contention that Martin would have an advantage in hot weather, but Martin told the court how irritating the two rubberized stockings can be in humid weather. "My leg sweats under that stocking and it becomes very abrasive," he said. "It's rubbed raw many times around my knee, around my foot. It's just extremely uncomfortable in hot weather because of the stocking and through the sweat."

"So do you see an advantage that you would have over a PGA Tour player, competitor of yours, in hot weather if you were allowed to ride a cart as opposed to them walking?" Wiswall asked.

"I don't see an advantage," Martin answered. "If I could trade my leg and a cart for that good leg, I'd do it anytime, anywhere." Throughout his testimony, Martin was emphatic but unemotional—until he started speaking about his college years. He started out at school "extremely active" and relatively problem-free his first two years, even while carrying his own bag for thirty-six holes in a single day. "However, over time that became extremely difficult for me," he said. "And I can remember when my leg was extremely bad my junior year. I remember an episode in, kind of—Arizona, and my leg had a horrible spell. And it was thirty-six holes, and I was in an extreme amount of pain. And I remember the coach for them, Randy Lyon, came up and said, 'Man, you've got to take a cart, please take it.' And I wouldn't do it."

At that moment, Martin signaled that he couldn't continue and reached for a tissue. His brother and mother were also in tears, and Judge Coffin declared a five-minute recess. When he got back on the stand, Wiswall asked him if he thought playing professionally would be easier since he'd have a caddie. "Yeah," Martin said. "In fact, after I graduated from college I was excited because I figured the tough part was done, you know, thirty-six holes carrying your bag."

Martin's testimony ended on a controversial note. Wiswall tried to ask him if he felt there was a similarity between the

148

There must have been many times during the trial that Martin daydreamed about his postponed golf career, even if it meant having to play the sport in part behind the wheel. Another heavy hitter on his side was Nike, as evidenced by the golf hat he's wearing. (AP/Wide World photo by Harry Cabluck)

no-cart rule and the Caucasian-only clause that was part of the PGA bylaws back in the sixties, but Maledon strongly objected to the question as inappropriate and irrelevant. Coffin agreed and sustained the objection.

Maledon was pretty easy on Martin in his cross-examination. "I know this is difficult for you," the attorney told him. "I'll try to be brief. I often say that, and it doesn't come to pass, but I'll try." His first line of attack concerned the three sets of rules Nike Tour players have to follow: the USGA, the local rules, and the so-called hard card that outlines the conditions of competition where the walking rule appears, among others, like the one-ball rule. "You don't get to pick and choose which one of those you're going to follow?" Maledon asked, rhetorically. "Now, you would agree with me, would you not, Mr. Martin, that if a rule applicable to a particular competition were changed for one competitor, but not for the other competitors, that that would fundamentally alter the nature of that competition, isn't that true, sir?"

"No," responded Martin, "I don't believe that."

Martin did agree, however, that changing the rule that limits contestants to fourteen clubs for one player but not others would fundamentally alter the game. "Well, certainly," he said. "Because that's shotmaking, that's where the game is played, with your clubs. And so if someone had an advantage with their clubs, I could see where that would be an alteration of the game."

Maledon then asked him to confirm that the Hooters Tour turned down his cart request, as did the USGA before, when he wanted to qualify for the 1997 U.S. Open. "I called one of the officials on the phone," said Martin, referring to the latter. "He rudely said no."

Finally, Maledon sought to establish that Martin was not an employee of the PGA Tour, which, if he were, it would be much harder for the tour to win its case. He presented Martin with the tour's IRS filing that showed he won $3,000 at the 1997 Q-School and indicated the money was paid under "non-employee compensation." He also showed him a copy of his check stub for the $40,000 he won at the Lakeland Classic, revealing that no state or federal tax was withheld. Maledon then established that Martin decides which tournaments he's going to play. The tour also doesn't tell him which brand of clubs he has to use, nor do they reimburse him for his travel expenses. Although they receive a stipend for health insurance, Nike Tour players don't have a retirement plan or disability benefits. It was clear that Martin was self-employed, as he indicated on his tax returns.

Martin's testimony ended on a light note when Wiswall presented the court with a three-and-a-half-minute video depicting Martin's use of a cart at the Lakeland tournament. "I'll warn you, this is a bad putt," Martin joked. When Judge Coffin asked if Maledon had any questions, the attorney said, "I want to cross-examine the witness about his putting stroke."

The final bit of testimony for Martin came in a ninety-minute videotaped deposition from Gerry Norquist, the former Eugene Country Club assistant pro who's played a lot of golf with Martin. He recalled the day when Martin was in pain after a round together and showed him his leg in the bag room one day. "I was a little bit shocked, actually," he said. "I find it hard to believe that anyone can do anything to give him a competitive advantage."

The PGA Tour was going to do its best to show how a cart would do just that when it began to present its side of the case.

CHAPTER NINE

Caught in the Legal Rough

As the case continued to attract national attention, Maledon and company went on the offensive. If they were going to save the PGA Tour, then the Senior Tour, which allows carts, would be the sacrificial lamb. The first witness to wield the knife was Richard Ferris, the former CEO of United Airlines and now the chairman of the tour's policy board. Ferris's relationship with the tour began in the mid-eighties when he was chairman of the policy board of the newly formed Senior Tour. What, Maledon wanted to know, are the differences between the Senior Tour and the other two tours?

"The Nike Tour and the regular tour are golf at its very highest level," he said. "The Senior Tour . . . it's nostalgic. What was being marketed on the Senior Tour were the names."

Names like Sam Snead, Julius Boros, and Arnold Palmer had dotted the Senior Tour's landscape. And if some of them couldn't walk as well as they used to, then they should be able to ride. "It's an economic matter," Ferris said. "If Arnold Palmer's got an arthritic hip and he can't walk eighteen holes, [we still] want Arnold Palmer out there playing because he's good for five thousand more people to show up at the tournament. He's a draw. He's an economic draw. That's why you allow them to use carts, because it's a nostalgia tour."

Based on what Ferris said, it seemed clear that the PGA Tour does not consider walking the course to be an integral part of the Senior Tour. The courses are also set up a lot easier. They're shorter with easier pin placements and less rough. "It's not golf at its highest level," added Ferris, who used the word *nostalgia* eleven times. "Everything we do on the regular tour and on the Nike Tour is golf at its very highest level. . . . [The Senior Tour] is a combination of nostalgia and competition." In saying what he said, Ferris, likely unwittingly, was about to unleash the fury of a number of seniors—Lee Trevino included—who see their tour as anything but "nostalgic."

In her cross-examination, Martha Walters noted that the Senior Tour had been called by many the most successful sports venture of the 1980s, and that it had grown in stature beyond all expectations, even though some of its members used carts. Two events in 1980 had grown to twenty-seven by 1985, the same year ESPN first televised seven events. The following year, Arnold Palmer tried to get carts banned from the tour because they detracted from the public image. He succeeded for a week or two until some of the less-than-mobile players rose up against it. "Arnold felt very strongly that walking is an integral physical part of the game," said Ferris, a business associate and close friend of Palmer's. "I should know that—he's told it to me enough times."

Ferris was kind in his comments about the Senior Tour compared to the tour's next witness, Ken Venturi, the highly respected CBS golf analyst and former touring pro. He said there's no comparison between the older guys and the younger players. "Let them do whatever they want. It's just an outing. . . . It's a round of golf at the club. It's a bunch of seniors getting together having a good time and making a million dollars. They love it. If they didn't have that, they'd be at a driving range or picking up balls."

Although his testimony was often disjointed, Venturi was a key witness for the defense, given his triumphant 1964 U.S. Open victory at Congressional Country Club in Washington, D.C., where he staggered to victory in one-hundred-degree heat and 95 percent humidity. He was out on the course for ten hours during the thirty-six-hole final and lost eight pounds. Not only did some players drop out, so did some of the gallery. He started the day six shots behind the leaders but made up considerable ground after shooting a 66 in the morning round (despite bogeying the last two holes). He was so dehydrated and exhausted, he was shaking. As Venturi lay disoriented on the locker-room floor during the break, sipping iced tea and downing salt tablets, a doctor told him if he went back out, it could be fatal. Venturi, who had been in a four-year slump, looked at the doctor and said, "It's better than the way I'm living. I got to go out there. I've been waiting for this day all my life."

And so he went out. "I had to go," he said, recounting the story on the stand. "I had no other place to go. I waited all my life for that moment."

While Venturi said fatigue is still a big factor on tour, even though the PGA Tour no longer plays thirty-six-hole finals, he

Ken Venturi. (PGA Tour photo)

had a hard time coming up with current examples where players struggled like he did at the Open. He mentioned the FedEx
Saint Jude Classic in June 1997 in Memphis, where the heat
was stifling. "Play was a little bit slower," he said. "They weren't
on the practice tee very long."

Nevertheless, Venturi said to allow one person to use a
cart would fundamentally alter the game. "If you take fatigue
and you can eliminate some of that and save one stroke, that's
the difference between winning a major championship and
finishing runner-up. One shot." But Venturi was a bit uncomfortable up on the stand, and wanted to make it clear he wasn't
against Martin. "I'm not here to go against Casey Martin," he
said. "I have the greatest respect and admiration for him. And
his talent, I think, is superb. . . . [But] where do you draw the

156

line? That's the part about it. It's not one person. Who does and who doesn't? How bad, how good, before you get one or don't get one. And then what you are doing now is changing the level of competition."

"I'm looking at carts," Venturi added a little later. "Again, please, this is not—I'm not dealing in personalities. I'm dealing in golf carts, because if I had my way, I wish that everything would be all right. I wish things could be better. I wish talent could—there weren't those things in the world. I really do. But that's not what I'm here for."

Wiswall picked up on Venturi's respect for Martin in his cross-examination. "I like him because he doesn't complain," Venturi said. "Excuses are crutches for the untalented." And even though Venturi admitted he didn't know much about Martin's medical condition, other than what he read in the paper, he admitted that Martin started at a disadvantage. "Think how good—if he didn't have it, just think how good he would be," he said, then looked at Martin, who was seated at his lawyer's table. "Is it your right leg?" Wiswall said it was. "Think if he could kick that leg in there and get that calf in there to pick up twenty more yards off the tee. . . ."

It was vital, as far as the tour was concerned, to keep the focus off Martin. They wanted the case to lean in a different direction. But this wasn't the American Civil Liberties Union suing the PGA Tour on behalf of some John or Jane Doe pro. The issue was whether a very sympathetic figure with a clearly defined disability would have an edge if he rode in a cart. That's why their best witness was another pro with a disability, Scott Verplank, who suffers from diabetes and has had three elbow operations. In his videotaped deposition, he said he couldn't understand why more golfers didn't use a cart at the

1997 qualifying tournament, which he won by six shots. After learning that Martin was going to get a cart at the Q-School, Verplank asked for one, too.

"It felt great, and I never got tired," he said. "I put extra water bottles in my cart, sat on that comfortable seat, put my legs up. I didn't understand why everybody wasn't using them. . . . I thought they were dumb for not riding." He added that it is fundamentally unfair for any golfer to use a cart, regardless of his or her limitations. "You can't give a kid a one-up [advantage] on the first tee. I have a debilitating disease, too. I'm just as disabled as he is."

The videotaped testimony of golf legends Jack Nicklaus and Arnold Palmer that followed proved anticlimactic, mainly because they went over issues that others had already discussed. Both asserted that walking is fundamental to championship-level golf and that a cart would give a player a competitive advantage. "[Carts] would take the physicalness out of the game—part of its tradition and integrity," said Palmer, who recalled how his own father, an accomplished golfer, had to overcome physical ailments that hampered his play. "Some people are unfortunately faced with physical difficulties, and my father happened to be one of them. My father might have played professional golf if he'd had two good legs, but he didn't, and so he didn't make it."

Palmer predicted doom if the PGA Tour were forced to respond to multiple requests for carts. "Where do you stop having people ride?" he asked. "If that happens, we may not have a tour at all. It may disappear."

If Martin were given a cart, Nicklaus said, echoing Palmer's comments, the sport could succumb to a debate over who is eligible for carts and who isn't. "We'd never get off the first tee,"

Jack Nicklaus and Arnold Palmer. (PGA Tour photos)

said the winner of eighteen professional majors, who also recounted how he sprained his ankle when he stepped on a pine cone during a recent round, but still insisted on walking "because that's the essence of playing the game."

On the fifth and final day of testimony, Judy Bell, the immediate past president of the USGA—and the only woman to testify during the trial—was the first witness to take the stand on behalf of the PGA Tour. An expert on the rules of the game, she focused her discussion on the optional conditions found in the appendix to the Rules of Golf. If the committee in charge of the competition adopts any of them, such as making players walk or use one type of ball, then they are every bit as sacrosanct as all the other rules.

Under cross-examination, Bell said the rules on the books making exceptions for disabled players were never meant to apply to professional golf. Wiswall presented her with a copy of a pamphlet entitled *A Modification of the Rules of Golf for Golfers with Disabilities*, which the USGA wrote along with the

Royal & Ancient Golf Club of St. Andrews and the Association of Disabled American Golfers. Wiswall noted that the book stated: "In modifying the rules of golf for golfers with disabilities, the desired result should allow the disabled golfer to play equitably with an able-bodied individual or a golfer with another type of disability." Bunkers, for example, don't exist for a wheelchair-bound player, since it would be very difficult to get in and out.

"That modification is for disabled players getting around the golf course, but it's not perceived to be adopted in top-level competition," said Bell, who admitted that, despite the language in the book, the modifications really couldn't be used for an able-bodied person to play a disabled person, at least competitively. "They apply to recreational golf."

Wiswall also raised some interesting points about the handicapping system, which the USGA oversees. "Your handicap system does not pose any penalty against a person who uses a cart, does it?" he asked.

"No, it doesn't," said Bell.

"Well, I was curious, though, if a cart provides such a fundamental advantage, why do you not, when you establish golfers' handicaps, assess a penalty against the ones who use a cart when they play, as opposed to those who walk?"

When Bell said she didn't know how you could keep track of whether people ride or walk, Wiswall suggested players could check a box at the bottom of a scorecard to indicate whether or not they used a cart. The USGA could then factor it in just like the slope, or course difficulty rating, is. But Bell disagreed. "I just don't think that's practical," she said.

The last witness to testify for the tour was Commissioner Tim Finchem, who, not surprisingly, was their most eloquent defender. Answering questions in complete thoughts and sentences, the former attorney, who had once been an economic advisor to President Jimmy Carter, was a trial lawyer's—and court reporter's—best friend. He first addressed familiar issues, such as why it's necessary that all competitors walk, and how giving one person a cart would fundamentally alter the nature of the competition. "It is no longer a level playing field," he said. "It's one playing field for this competitor and a different playing field for everybody else."

Finchem's most interesting comments related to the small disparity between the top players on tour and the also-rans, so even the slightest advantage could have a huge impact. For his slide-show illustration, he cited Martin's former Stanford teammate, Tiger Woods, who was the No. 1 money winner in 1997; and Craig Parry, who finished sixty-third on the money list. The difference between Woods's scoring average (69.1) and Parry's (70.17) was one stroke per round. That small difference amounted to a substantial dollar differential, however: $1.6 million, or about $80,000 per event. Another graph showed that if a player averaged just two strokes higher a round, his earnings dropped to about $250,000.

"When we talk about changing a rule to provide for one player or some subset of players, you have to take into consideration what it does to the overall fairness and equity of the competition with regard to all the other players," he said. "And in looking at this particular case with regard to walking, it's not just that walking is important—an important part of the sport. It's not just that the athleticism of walking is part of the sport. It's not just that we have different rules for different people which inherently, in our judgment, changes the concept of a level playing field for athletics, but also we are a professional sport. We are a sport where the competitors are earning a living, and we also believe it would not be fair to the other competitors in the field to have a special set of rules for one player or some subset of players."

The Billy Andrade example, introduced at the trial, was perhaps an even more telling example of how much difference one stroke can make. By finishing five dollars out of the top thirty on the 1997 money list, Andrade missed playing in the Tour Championship, where he would have made at least $64,000 even if he came in last, and could have earned $750,000 if he won. He also would have gained automatic entry into the 1998 Masters and U.S. Open. "There's probably forty different rounds of golf he played, maybe more, where one shot, all year long, would have made the difference between him finishing thirty-first and thirtieth," Finchem said.

While Finchem agreed that there's no way to quantify the competitive advantage a competitor would get if a particular rule were waived, he pointed out under cross-examination that Verplank and Martin both won recent tournaments in carts. "I can only assume that some would have the perception that a golf cart creates an advantage," he said. "That's one of the difficulties of this issue; it's impossible to measure."

No issue was left unexplored, even whether the tour would change its motto from "Anything's Possible" to "These Guys are Good" because of Martin. "No, absolutely not," said Finchem. "The history on this change goes back a year and a half." A more obvious question was whether the case was an important one to the tour. "Yes, absolutely. If it wasn't important, if it wasn't an integral part of competition, certainly we would have found a way to settle this matter and provide an exception and move on, rather than expend the time and energy of all these folks over weeks and weeks of depositions and trial."

Even though he had refused to view Martin's medical records, Finchem concluded by saying he accepted Martin's argument that he cannot walk eighteen holes. "I've talked to him about it personally. I understand where he's coming from, and I know that the best medical advice in the world is telling him that he just cannot play this game at this level and be able to walk. I understand all that. And as difficult as it is, we have to go past that and recognize the impact on the sport to making a special exception."

Perhaps the most telling statement of the day came not from Finchem, Maledon, Wiswall, or Walters, but from Judge Coffin, who indicated that after closing arguments the following morning, they would reconvene at 3:00 P.M., prompting speculation that he would issue his ruling. Had he already made up his mind? Apparently so, and it didn't look good for the tour. Speaking to reporters afterward, Finchem didn't seem optimistic. He complained that the decision was being made "by individuals who, frankly, don't have any background in [golf], and that is bothersome."

The tour was taking it on the chin, not just from a general public that had a hard time understanding their rigid position, but from some of its own member players as well. It's one thing for critics to deride the Senior Tour as "geezer golf," but when the PGA Tour did it itself, that didn't sit too well with some of its members. "My opinion of the nostalgic tour is [a lot of bunk]," Palmer told *Golf Digest*. "In the early days, we did try to keep some of the older, more well-known players out there to attract attention. But that time has passed."

The lawsuit and ensuing trial took a heavy toll emotionally on Martin, who went back to the Nike Tour after the trial trying to piece his game back together. It wasn't easy. (Chris Pietsch/the *Register-Guard*)

Lee Trevino was even more forceful. "First of all, if Richard Ferris knew the difference between nostalgia and competition, he'd still be running United Airlines," he said. "We take his comments as a real low blow. I'm very disturbed about it, because this gentleman happens to be on our board. And if that's the kind of talk coming from our board, I think we should get another board member."

By the end of the trial, Martin was emotionally spent. His Hooters Tour companion John Sosa spoke to him by phone the day before the verdict. "I asked him what he thought might happen and he said, 'I have no clue. I hope they rule in my favor, but it could go either way,' " Sosa says. "He felt like he had a chance. He didn't feel like he was out of it. But he said, 'At this point, I just want to get it over with. I'm tired.' He was completely exhausted. He couldn't wait for it to be over so he could get back to concentrating on golf."

It had been a long journey for Martin. There had been a time in the not-too-distant past, when he refused to even acknowledge he had a disability, and he would rather have played through excruciating pain than give in to the offer of a lift. Now, the self-effacing Martin had emerged as not only the ADA poster boy, but as a golfer actually demanding use of a cart. His change in sentiment hadn't been easy on him. Two aspects in particular bothered him about the case. "One, I don't want to be known as a handicapped kid who got a cart," he told his former South Eugene High teammate Austin Teague. "I want to be known for my accomplishments on the golf course." He was also troubled by the testimony of Nicklaus and Palmer.

"Casey and I both were big fans of Jack Nicklaus, the greatest player to ever play, and Arnold Palmer, the most

popular player to ever play," Teague says. "Growing up as little boys, both of us playing golf at twelve years old and idol-
izing these guys, to see them talk out against Casey is something that hurt him."

Palmer and Nicklaus received a lot of angry letters for the
positions they took. Martin had already won in the court of
public opinion; now he was about to find out if he would in
the court that mattered most.

CHAPTER TEN

Ticket to Ride

The biggest day of Martin's life dawned cold and gray. This was the day he would find out what he would be doing for the rest of his life, or at least the rest of the life of his leg. No doubt about it, his leg was dying, as Walters said in her closing argument. The summations provided a sharp contrast in styles. Quoting Albert Schweitzer and Martin Luther King Jr., Walters went for the inspirational and the emotional. Quoting from case law, Maledon forcefully went for the legal and the logical.

"Casey Martin would not be here if it meant that he were asking for anything, anything extra," said Walters, who immediately took issue with the tour's contention that Martin's condition shouldn't be a factor. "We say that this case is about Casey Martin for the sole reason that this case has to be about Casey Martin under the law of this land, because individualized decision-making is the essence, the fundamental nature of the ADA."

She spoke about "affirmative accommodation" with regard to the disabled. "Equal treatment is not sufficient when we are talking about the disabled," she said. "The government has to make exceptions to its laws, employers have to make exceptions to their rules, and public accommodations have to make exceptions to their eligibility requirements."

In the case of the PGA Tour, she argued that one of those requirements—walking—was not fundamental to the sport. "Mr. Finchem and Mr. Palmer and Mr. Venturi both said that Casey Martin is an excellent player," she said. "His talent is superb. What do they mean? Could you say about a basketball player that he is an excellent player if he couldn't run, or a weight lifter if he couldn't lift? They are saying that about him because he is excellent at the primary things that it takes to do the job. . . . The position of a professional golfer does not exist to walk. It exists to make shots with a club and ball."

In the thirty years the PGA Tour has existed in its modern incarnation, never once have they tested a player for his walking abilities. She noted, in fact, that whenever it's "administratively convenient," they allow carts, such as in the first two stages of tour school and for shuttles between the ninth green and the tenth tee at certain golf courses. She jumped on the rule's inconsistency. "It says you shall walk at all times unless riding is permitted by the rules committee. It has built-in flexibility. If it were essential, you'd have to do it always. You wouldn't—you can't play basketball without dribbling. You couldn't say you shall dribble at all times except when permitted by a rules committee."

She didn't buy into the argument that the tour was testing rigor with its walking requirement. "Why do you play eighteen holes when you used to play thirty-six?" she asked. "In 1976

Arthur Daley wrote in the *New York Times* the stamina has been removed from the game. Only the skill remains." Nor did she believe that it would fundamentally alter their tournaments to have one person ride. "This is not a class-action suit. . . . We are not asking that anyone other than Casey Martin ride. We are asking that they let Casey Martin right here, this one guy with a dying leg, have a ride part of the way."

Finally, she contended that the tour didn't offer any proof that Martin would have a competitive advantage if he rode. "The only way that there could possibly be an advantage would be if the exertion by walking—by those who walk over Casey Martin riding—brought on more fatigue. But there is no able-bodied person that's going to get more fatigued than Casey Martin. . . . We submit that one should say Casey Martin has chalk on his shoes [i.e., cheats] unless that person looks at his dying leg and listens to his doctor and learns about fatigue. No one who did so could look him in the eye and say, honestly, you are an excellent golfer, but we will not let you play because we require stamina and you don't demonstrate it. He does. He deserves a chance. . . . We are seeking an equal opportunity for Mr. Martin to demonstrate his abilities. . . . Mr. Martin just needs a ride to the starting line. He's not asking for a fifty-yard lead. The ADA vision is of an America where persons are judged by their abilities, not on the basis of their disabilities."

Maledon's tone in his closing argument was so strong and indignant that some courtroom observers were taken aback. He repeatedly reminded Judge Coffin of what his job was, and even went so far as to admonish him not to let public sympathy for Martin sway his decision. He was resolute in his feelings that the law was on the tour's side. "Plaintiff's counsel has consistently misstated the applicable law to the court and has repeatedly urged the court to make rulings that would clearly be wrong as a matter of law," Maledon said at the outset. "Your Honor has to decide where the focus is. If Your Honor agrees with the plaintiff, that the focus is broader than just the PGA Tour and the Nike Tour competitions, then I submit that this case is going to be decided on a basis that—for which there is no legal support whatsoever."

He wanted Judge Coffin to ignore all the evidence about the use of carts in college, qualifying tournaments, and the Senior Tour. "The ADA requires the court to examine the particular accommodation to which the plaintiff seeks access, not other accommodations in the same general category," Maledon said. "The court should not, and I submit to you, you can't focus on the Senior Tour, because that's not where access is being sought, and what is done at the Senior Tour, and the reasons for doing it at the Senior Tour, are irrelevant to the determination that the court has to make."

It was also irrelevant whether walking was a fundamental rule of golf. What mattered was whether it was a fundamental rule of the PGA Tour. He compared it to the three-point line in the NBA. "Your Honor can't tell me that there is any book on basketball that says a three-point line is fundamental. But I submit to you, Your Honor, that if a court were to issue a ruling saying that a particular handicapped individual did not need to adhere to the three-point line, it would fundamentally alter the nature of NBA basketball, because it's a purposeful rule of NBA basketball. That's the standard that the court has to apply. Not whether it's a fundamental rule, but whether it would fundamentally alter the nature of the accommodation to which access is sought."

Time and again, Maledon cited case law to support his position, which he interpreted to say the ADA forbade the court from requiring a fundamental alteration in the tour's regulations to accommodate a disabled person. In one case, the court said it was unreasonable to allow a father to assist his disabled son while on the ice playing hockey. "No case has ever held that the ADA requires a sports organization to accommodate a disabled competitor by exempting him from a substantive rule of competition applicable to all," Maledon said. "If the ADA requires professional sports organizations to accommodate disabled competitors by exempting them from the substantive rules of the competition, competitions as we know them will cease to exist. It's that simple."

As far as the PGA Tour was concerned, walking was not just for the sake of the TV cameras; it's a rule with real substance that enhances the competition by injecting a fatigue element into it. It's not one of style, like the one requiring tour pros to wear collared shirts, argued Maledon. By indicating that prior cases didn't allow the court to make an "individualized determination," Maledon beseeched Judge Coffin not to consider the fatigue factor when comparing Martin to able-bodied players. Every athlete brings to the sport a different skill level. "You don't try to compensate for those differences in ability," Maledon said, comparing a disability to a lack of talent to drive the ball a long way.

Granting Martin use of a cart might or might not, he continued, give Martin an advantage, and that's the problem. "This whole issue of competitive advantage is not one that Your Honor can decide conclusively. . . . The fact that people who put on the PGA Tour events believe in good faith that use of a cart reduces the fatigue factor and takes away one of the elements that they want as part of their competition, that's all Your Honor needs to know."

Maledon closed by acknowledging the vast amount of public sympathy accorded Martin, which he understood. "I think Mr. Martin is an outstanding individual and I've said that from the time I first met him. But that's not what this case is about. . . . The right thing to do would be to decide this case in accordance with the applicable law and not on the basis of public sentiment."

Martin must have felt pretty good about the way the day had gone. During a break in the closing arguments, he was seen practicing his swing in the hallway. Maybe he would have a pro career after all. Judge Coffin deliberated just a few hours. When he took the bench at 3:00 P.M. on Wednesday, February 11, one of the first issues he addressed was the sympathy vote. "I want to assure everyone that the court does not decide cases based upon sympathy, nor does the court decide cases based upon the prestige of any of the parties," he said to a packed courtroom hanging on his every word. "I took an oath when I became a judge to decide cases based upon the law and the facts, and I've always done my best to do exactly that."

After acknowledging that both parties had strong positions and that the case would have "significant precedential impact," he complimented both sides on their presentations. He then gave a discourse on the ADA. "Congress intended to protect disabled persons not just from intentional discrimination, but also from thoughtlessness, indifference, and benign neglect," he said, adding that Martin did indeed fit the definition of disabled. What he didn't fit, however, was the definition of an employee, so he wasn't entitled to that specific accommodation under that section of the ADA. That was good news for the

PGA, but that was about it. Judge Coffin did the very thing they feared most: He would look at other examples, such as the NCAA and the Senior Tour, to decide that the use of a cart was a reasonable modification. Another strong factor, he said, was that the USGA rules do not *require* walking.

The onus then shifted to the tour, which had to convince the judge that a cart request would fundamentally alter the nature of its competitions. He agreed that walking was a substantive rule, not one of style, but disagreed with the tour when it came to considering Martin's particular condition. "With respect to the fatigue factor, under normal circumstances, from the evidence I've heard, walking an eighteen-hole course, five to six miles in the four- to five-hour time period, with intervals of rest and opportunities for refreshment, it's not significantly taxing," Judge Coffin said. "There are circumstances where it can be taxing, certainly. But significantly taxing? I don't agree with that. Walking, like breathing, is natural for the able-bodied."

Casey Martin, on the other hand, comes to the course with the fatigue factor built in. "It's clear that fatigue from his leg condition is easily greater than the fatigue a normal person undergoes by walking the course. Easily," said the judge. "I don't find that to be an impossible decision to make, by any means." Thus, Martin already met the purpose of the rule, so granting him a cart was a reasonable modification, at least in his specific case. "As a result, I find that the PGA Tour has not met its burden of proving that the modification would fundamentally alter the nature of its Nike Tour competition.

"And I want to stress that there is—I've heard evidence from some of the witnesses, I think Mr. Palmer was one—that this would be the end of PGA Tour golf as it is known. That's clearly not the case. Granting a cart to Mr. Martin does not mean in any way, shape, or form that anyone else out there has some right to a cart. Any perception that he has unfair advantage by riding a cart, as I've said, is wrong. Mr. Martin is entitled to his modification because he is disabled. It will not alter what's taking place out there on the course."

Martin nodded emphatically several times as Judge Coffin announced his decision. When Coffin was finished, many of the spectators applauded. After exchanging hugs with his two attorneys and family, Martin let out a single whoop of relief. Wiswall obviously had high confidence they would win. Right after the ruling he passed out buttons that said, "I Can . . . with

In one of the most emotional moments of his young life, Martin appears at a news conference following his courtroom victory. Seated behind him, left to right, are his parents and brother—King, Melinda, and Cam. (Chris Pietsch/the *Register-Guard*)

a Cart," alluding to the Nike slogan. Walters emerged from the courthouse into a phalanx of cameras. She couldn't contain her glee as she walked down the street with her two children. "It means a career for one person and hope for millions more," she told reporters, and then praised her client. "To never complain, to never, ever ask, 'Are we going to win?' To take whatever life dishes out to you. I'll try to remember that all my life. I'm very honored to be a part of this."

An hour later, after changing out of his blue shirt and blue blazer to a Nike golf shirt, Martin held a press conference at the nearby Hilton. Flanked by his family, lawyers, and business representatives, Martin fought back the tears as he tried to thank his supporters, including Jesus Christ, Phil Knight, and ADA author Sen. Tom Harkin. "I didn't want to do this," he said, struggling to contain his emotions in front of a dozen or more cameras. "It's been a tough time, but also a great time. I can't believe this is really me up here. . . . I just hope maybe five or ten years from now, if I'm still able to play golf, the PGA Tour will kind of lean back and scratch their heads and say, 'Now, why did we fight this guy?' I just want to be given a chance to play. Believe me, I wouldn't have done this if I thought I had an advantage [using a cart]."

The turning point in the trial, he thought, was the tour's refusal to consider his medical condition. He had a hard time understanding the tour's position that the case wasn't about him. "What do they mean the case wasn't about Casey Martin," he said. "I'm the one with the disability. I'm the one suing you." He also said he didn't hold any grudges against the tour and that his biggest worry had now shifted from the trial to succeeding under all the scrutiny. "I'm not Tiger Woods yet. I could go down in flames with everyone watching. But this does allow me to pursue my dreams."

Hollywood, of course, was already calling for the movie rights. He might agree, he joked, "as long as Tom Cruise plays my part." (Another suggestion might be Matthew Perry, one of the six co-stars of the popular TV sitcom *Friends*— Perry is almost a dead ringer for Martin, both in the face and tall, lanky build.)

The happy ending Hollywood likes so much could end up on the cutting-room floor, since the tour immediately vowed to appeal the decision. There's some merit to their argument that the ADA doesn't apply to the area inside the ropes, especially in common-sense terms, since the ropes are used to, literally, keep out the public.

"The PGA Tour is disappointed with the decision," Commissioner Tim Finchem said in a statement. "As we have said from the outset of this lawsuit, we believe firmly in the basic premise of any sport, that one set of rules must be applied equally to all competitors. Additionally, we believe strongly in the central role walking plays for all competitors in tournament championship golf at the PGA Tour and Nike Tour levels."

Needless to say, the verdict was a controversial one, and reaction from players, as well as legal experts, ran the gamut. Bobby Silverstein, the director of the Center for the Study and Advancement of Disability Policy at the George Washington University Medical Center, called the decision critical. "It's about empowering people with disabilities," he told *Golf World*. "That's why Casey Martin is so important."

But Scott Mills, a Washington, D.C., employment law attorney, said the Oregon court had stretched the application of the ADA far beyond its original intent. "Congress never intended that the ADA would require professional sporting associations to amend their rules to accommodate members of the public who otherwise are physically restricted in their ability to compete in a sport," he wrote in the *Baltimore Sun*. "Nor did Congress intend for the ADA to require public access to the competitive area of a professional sporting event while the event is in progress."

The tour was in Honolulu for the Hawaiian Open when the decision came down. "It's a huge black eye [for the tour]," golfer Paul Goydos said. "I think that's what going to linger most—not whether he walks or rides, or what happens in the appeals process, but the perception that we're a bunch of ogres."

Tom Watson was worried about the ruling's implications, however. "As much compassion as I have for Casey, I have contempt for the decision, that [the tour] cannot make its own rules. If you can really make a narrow decision based on Casey's case individually, it's fine. But when you open up the door to Casey, you open up the door to Bill Glasson, J. C. Snead, Scott Verplank, Fred Couples, and all the others who could use the carts. You open up the door. I don't think that door should be open at all."

When do chronic ailments become permanent disabilities? Not long after the trial ended, Ed Fiori had to withdraw from the Honda Classic because of his nagging injuries. The veteran pro, who ended a fourteen-year losing streak at Quad Cities in 1996 (when he outdueled Tiger Woods), suffers from a decaying disk in his back and a pinched nerve in his foot. "Hell, yes, I want a buggy," he said at Doral. "It's a definite advantage. I can't play because I can't walk." But he didn't find any support from other players or tour officials. "They're going to vote down any extra carts," he said. "I asked [the tour], 'What can I do to get a cart?' They said, 'You have to sue us.' I haven't decided to

The media circus didn't end with the Oregon trial. It kept right on trucking, following Martin to Austin, Texas, for his first official tournament since the trial. (AP/Wide World photo by Harry Cabluck)

do that, but my lawyer told me it's a case of win-win-win. I'd hate to quit for medical reasons. I have a disability."

Still, Martin's situation is unique. Even pros with persistent injuries have hope that they can be corrected. Jose Maria Olazabal's foot problems kept him from playing for two years, but a doctor finally solved his problem. Martin has no hope, and the PGA Tour missed a golden PR opportunity. "We should have given him a cart because there aren't going to be many other disabled golfers who will qualify for the tour in the next twenty, thirty years," says Peter Jacobsen, who attended the University of Oregon and has known Martin since he was twelve. "We're not going to have a blind golfer out there or somebody in a wheelchair. I don't know why we put it in the hands of the court to begin with. We should have just kept it in-house and given him a cart."

Even if the liberal Ninth Circuit Court in San Francisco overturns the ruling, that could take a year or two. In the meantime, Martin can continue to pursue his dream. The toughest part of the trial for him was the ten-day wait to find out if he still had a professional golf career or not. Right after the trial ended, he moved out of his parents' house to a town-house near his alma mater so he could use the school's prac-tice facilities. El Niño notwithstanding, the weather's better, too. Had it gone the other way, Martin would have been liable for the tour's attorneys' fees, estimated at $1 million. He would have had to declare bankruptcy, but it's doubtful the PGA Tour would have gone after him since it wouldn't have looked so good. He was also off the hook for Wiswall's and Walters's fees and expenses, which were nearly $500,000, according to court filings. The court ordered the tour to pay about $227,000.

A better friend than Wiswall he could not have. "I didn't take this case because of money, and I didn't care if I ever got any money for the case," Wiswall says. "Casey was lucky. A lot of people who suffer from discrimination under the Americans with Disabilities Act cannot get competent counsel" because they can't afford to pay.

"As far as the ADA is concerned," Wiswall adds, "I'm slightly disillusioned about the rights of disabled persons to get skilled representation. When they fight against someone like Bill Maledon who, I'm sure, commands a premium dollar-per-hour fee, they must understand they might end up with a legal aid attorney."

The legal issues were behind Martin. Now it was time to get back to golf. The trial interfered with his play for almost a month, so he was naturally anxious about teeing up at the next Nike Tour stop in Austin a couple of weeks later with all the accompanying attention.

"U.S. Magistrate Thomas Coffin has blessed me with wings of opportunity . . . [but] I'm struggling a little bit with the expectations," he wrote in *Golf World*. "I know the world is watching. . . . No way in a thousand years could I have anticipated all that has happened in the last couple of months. What people have to remember is, this is all new to me, too. My life changed all at once and I'm grateful for that, but I can't say I'm truly prepared for it.

"There's one thing I want to make perfectly clear: I hold absolutely no hard feelings against the PGA Tour. There's no reason for me to gloat, no reason for me to wag my finger or say I beat them. I've said all along: The people who understand my physical condition know I don't gain a competitive advantage on the rest of the field. . . . I never felt overly confident about winning the case, and I'm not about to get cocky now. All I ever wanted was the opportunity to compete, and the PGA Tour, even if it was against its best wishes, appears ready to accommodate me. Thank goodness for that."

180

CHAPTER ELEVEN

Playing Through

In a way, the PGA Tour is lucky that it lost the case. Imagine the outcry had Martin broken his bad leg at his first post-trial tournament in Austin—because he had been forced by the tour to walk? Even if he had made it around by walking all four rounds, the sight of him limping on the evening news wouldn't have helped the tour's image one bit. The press followed his every move, even when he visited the loo, so any misstep would have been dutifully captured.

Nothing about Martin went unnoticed, including his new endorsement deals with Ping clubs and Hartford Life. The insurance company's name and logo (a big buck deer) appear just below his name on his giant Ping staff bag. It might seem like he was sticking it to the tour by signing a deal with Ping, but that's not the case. Those are the clubs he's always used, but there's no doubt the club manufacturer took perverse pleasure in signing Martin, given the vitriol of their lawsuit with the tour. Martin also signed a deal to play Top-Flight Strata Tour balls.

His agent, Chris Murray of Minneapolis-based Signature Sports Group, has to walk a thin line between fulfilling his fiduciary responsibility to Martin in getting him deals and not engendering any animosity among the Nike Tour's rank and file. "The last thing he wants to create is any resentment relative to his condition, and that would be the first thing somebody would run with," Murray told the *Register-Guard*.

About forty other companies have approached him offering endorsements, including those that produce medical products, food supplements, special beds, and bottled water. Martin is looking for companies that reflect his image and values, and Martin has since signed deals with Naya water and agreed to be a contributing editor of *We*, a lifestyle magazine for people with disabilities. You won't find Martin endorsing a golf-cart company, however, since he wants to focus people's attention away from that.

Fortunately, in Austin, Martin had an old friend to lean on. His Hooters Tour buddy John Sosa makes his home there. It was the first time they had seen each other since Martin had filed the lawsuit. Sosa called him a week before the Austin tournament to see if he wanted to stay with him—an invitation Martin would have jumped at in the past. Now, Martin had a place to stay right on the course and his schedule was already booked solid. He began his week at 4:30 A.M. on Monday (2:30 California time) to do a live interview with Matt Lauer on the *Today* show. He spent the rest of the day with Lauer's NBC colleague Stone Phillips at Barton Creek Country Club playing golf and doing an interview for *Dateline*.

Martin's first tournament back after the trial was the Nike Tour's Greater Austin Open in Texas. Here he pitches to the eighth green during the pro-am, with his caddie Steve Burdick watching. (AP/Wide World photo by Harry Cabluck)

"Man, it's just a zoo out there," Martin told Sosa. "You wouldn't believe it. I'm so busy, I can't even think straight. I get thirty to forty messages a day. I screen all my calls, but I'm going nuts!"

Sosa told him, "Hang in there, it can't last forever," to which Martin said, "Yeah, but it's just all at once."

"He didn't have time for anything else," Sosa says. "I asked him what he was going to do when he got to Austin, and he reeled off this schedule, and I was like, 'My goodness! When do you have time to eat and sleep?' He goes, 'I don't!' "

When they finally saw one another at the course during a practice round, Martin and Sosa exchanged hugs in front of all the news cameras, and Martin said, "John, you've got to help me with my swing. Tell me what I'm doing wrong, because I haven't played much golf and I need some help with my driver."

With the eyes of the golfing world on him, Martin needed to find his swing, and fast. The two used to help each other out with swing faults all the time on the Hooters Tour, so Sosa knew what to look for.

"He was sliding a little bit in front of the ball, which is understandable because he doesn't want to keep a lot of weight on his right side very long, so that is one of his swing flaws," Sosa says. "I was just trying to get him to feel like he stayed a little bit longer on his right foot before he hit the ball." The slide collapsed in the triangle formed by his arms, shoulders, and chest, causing Martin to block it right. Sosa stood perpendicular to him and held a club out horizontally with the butt-end up against the left side of Martin's head as he swung.

"His natural shot is a draw, a long one, too," Sosa adds. "So I said, 'Look, just keep your triangle firm and feel like it stays a little bit behind the ball on impact.' And he started ripping it. He was like, 'Oh my god, that's it, that's it!' He felt like, 'Man, this is kind of like old times, using one of our old remedies.' I think it kind of jazzed him up a little bit."

Sosa and his wife finally got to see Martin socially Saturday night, when they had him over for dinner with a number of other players. Sosa cooked his popular Thai peanut chicken. The good food and fellowship allowed Martin to relax for the first time in days. He was relieved to almost have the week behind him. By the time Sosa hooked up with him a month later in mid-April at the Nike Tour stop in Shreveport, Louisiana, Martin's life was finally getting back to some semblance of normality.

"I asked him how it was going and he said, 'Well, it's slowing down. I can breathe, it's not so bad. I can finally concentrate and play some golf. It's so much better.' He was more relaxed. He looked more like the regular Casey I knew."

Martin's life will never be normal again, though. Whether he likes it or not, he is now a bona fide celebrity. After the Shreveport tournament, where he missed his second cut in a row, Martin returned home to Foster City, California, to throw out the first pitch at a San Francisco Giants game. Manager Dusty Baker and pitcher Orel Hershiser are big fans of his. After Martin received some pointers from Baker in the clubhouse, the team mascot, a seal named Lou, drove Martin to the mound in a golf cart. To make him feel at home, Lou even planted a flagstick at home plate. It didn't do any good. It would be kind to say he bounced the ball in the dirt; it actually landed in the grass. One local sportscaster called it "the worst ceremonial pitch in San Francisco Giant history."

"Everybody warned me and said, 'You're going to throw it in the dirt,' " Martin recalled afterward. "I said, 'No, I won't.' I did. I just flat short-armed it." (To be fair, baseball was one of the few sports he didn't play growing up.)

Martin might be in the minor leagues of golf right now, but the Nike Tour is like Triple-A ball. He's just a phone call away from getting called up to the majors. After his court victory, Martin smartly declined invites to play in the Tucson Chrysler Classic and the Doral Ryder Open.

"I called to congratulate him, and he told me he had turned down some tournament sponsors and their spots," fellow Oregonian and pro golfer Peter Jacobsen says. "I told him I thought that was a good idea, because if he did take a couple of spots, he would be knocking out players who did qualify at the tour school. He said, 'I didn't qualify, they did. I'm only getting sponsors' spots because I won a lawsuit against the tour.' I agreed. He also said he wants to qualify for the tour from the Nike money list, so he has his head on straight. There's no doubt about it."

It didn't take long for the case to have a ripple effect. Although the USGA decided not to oppose Martin after the tour lost and allowed him to use a one-rider cart at sectional qualifying on June 8 at Clovernook Country Club in Cincinnati, they did deny another disabled golfer's request. Ford Olinger has a condition in both hips similar to what ended Bo Jackson's career. After his lawyer filed a motion asking for a temporary injunction, a federal judge in Fort Wayne, Indiana, granted an exemption to Olinger to use a cart in a local U.S. Open qualifier in mid-May. (He shot an 83 and failed to advance but has said he will pursue his lawsuit.)

Using a cart would seem like a simple matter, but it's not. It took Bill Wiswall and the tour two months to iron out a cart

During the week of the Austin tournament, Martin meets up with another pioneer in golf for the disabled—Colorado resident Greg Jones, founder and president of the Association of Disabled American Golfers. (AP/Wide World photo by L. M. Otero)

agreement. "The cart agreement has been particularly difficult for the parties," Wiswall wrote in court papers. "The parties had difficulty with the issue of how fast the cart could be operated, where it could be operated, how far ahead of the ball Mr. Martin could operate the cart and, on the speed issue, whether he would be entitled to operate it at a speed faster than walk speed, particularly if there was a problem with the gallery in the operation of the cart."

The tour also wanted the right to impose penalties against him if he violated the agreement and provide him with a different type of transportation than the standard golf cart. They eventually dropped both points. Still, Martin had to sign an eleven-point stipulation that included prohibitions against operating the cart at a speed faster than walking at a normal pace. He couldn't place endorsement logos on the cart, nor could the cart have a top or windshield or other accessory to provide protection from the elements. The tour also retained the right to keep him on the cart path if they decided that using it on the course could cause damage.

"I didn't think we need these rules, but I don't anticipate any problems," Martin told *USA Today*. "A lot got taken out. I wouldn't sign anything that was going to be a problem."

But there have been. At the Nike Carolina Classic in May, several players and caddies rode carts between the eighteenth green and the first tee. When Martin asked if his caddie, Steve Burdick, could have a ride, a rules official said no because there was a "no caddie" clause in the agreement. During the third round, Martin stood on the cart to see if the group ahead was still on the eighth green. Was it okay? Yes, said a rules official, but Martin feels like he's driving on eggshells at times.

When will we see a cart out on the PGA Tour for the first time? The best chance (at press time) appears to be in July at the Canon Greater Hartford Open or the CVS Charity Classic, although he qualified for the U.S. Open in June. The tournament Casey must really be looking forward to playing, though, will come in late September when the Nike Tour makes a pit stop in Eugene at Shadow Hills Country Club, where Martin has played many rounds. If he wins that and one other Nike Tour tournament, he will immediately receive a "battlefield promotion" to the PGA Tour; otherwise, he has to finish in the top fifteen on the money list to get his PGA Tour card for 1999.

His leg has become so painful lately, however, that it's really starting to affect his sleep more than ever before and, thus, his golf game. After winning $40,000 in his first event of the year, he made just $14,723 in his next nine events and didn't have one top-ten, leaving him ninth on the money list. There's no question he can play on the PGA Tour, but can he play for very long? It's obvious that even with a cart, he gets more fatigued than his competitors who are, of course, walking. But his problem, insofar as keeping up with his fellow pros, really comes after the round. When he should be beating balls on the range, Martin has to be resting his leg. The Nike Tour is too competitive for him not to practice as much as the other guys.

"I used to practice more when my leg felt better, but these days a round of golf is about all I can handle," Martin said at the Nike Carolina Classic in May. "The leg's getting worse. I don't think it's going to last much longer."

In the meantime, he's going to make the most of it. "Golf means very much to him; otherwise, he would not have pursued it the way he has," lifelong friend Austin Teague says. "He would not have taken the PGA Tour head-on. It was a bold move that not a lot of people have the guts to do. The PGA Tour is a powerful organization.

"Then again, with his faith in God, he is such a strong Christian man that golf is not the whole world to him. He knows there is a chance some day that he may not be able to play golf competitively because of his disability. I know he realizes that, and I think he has come to grips with that. The bottom line is he has so many talents that, even if he had to stop playing golf tomorrow, he would still be very successful in life. That's the kind of person he is."

"It was the first time I'd ever seen him really stand up for himself like that, because he was always such the nice guy," says another old friend, Sadie Ungemach. "I just love that he did it and was so strong. I'm so happy he won the case, but even if he didn't, the fact that he did it really just says a lot about Casey."

Before he moved to Foster City after the trial, Martin gave a moving speech to the youth group at Eugene's First Baptist Church on how his faith has helped him through his life.

"He gave a wonderful talk. I wish I had it on tape," youth pastor Rudy Herr says. "He was very articulate and gave all the credit for his strength to his relationship with God. He stressed how important that faith has been to him all of his life, especially through college and this past year.

"He knows his disability is something to be used to make him a strong person so he can be an inspiration to others who have disabilities. God has not given him a verbal answer why he had to be born with this birth defect, but he has had peace in his heart for a long time that God loves him and that God doesn't make junk."